D1829265

The Novel Today 1967-1975

RONALD HAYMAN

Published for the British Council
by Longman Group Ltd

Longman Group Ltd
Longman House, Burnt Mill, Harlow, Essex
Associated companies, branches and
representatives throughout the world

First published 1976
© Ronald Hayman

Printed in Great Britain
by W & J Mackay Limited, Chatham
by photo-litho

ISBN 0 528 01261 9

The opinions expressed in this booklet are the author's, and not necessarily those of the British Council

Contents

ERRATUM
Please note ISBN incorrec
0 582 01261

Illustrations

1

Realism and experiment are not antithetical

B. S. JOHNSON ANN QUIN DAVID PLANTE
CHRISTINE BROOKE-ROSE BRIGID BROPHY
GABRIEL JOSIPOVICI

When Ivy Compton-Burnett died in 1969, the Literary Editor of a leading weekly invited Anthony Powell to write a tribute to her. At first he demurred. A great English novelist had just died, he was told; he was the only great novelist among her survivors. How could he refuse?

Some critics maintain that none of our novelists deserves the word 'great'. Even on the question of who comes nearest to qualifying for it, there has never been more room for disagreement. Anthony Powell, Graham Greene, Angus Wilson, Iris Murdoch and William Golding could all find champions, while other critics could plausibly back Muriel Spark, Doris Lessing, John Fowles, V. S. Naipaul or Kingsley Amis, with the argument that no one is writing better. Other critics would argue that all these are too traditionalist, that none of them is taking enough risks.

According to Alain Robbe-Grillet, realistic story-telling has falsified the world of objects by humanizing them. 'It has become impossible to narrate', he insists in *Towards a New Novel* (1962). 'The exigencies of the anecdote were less compelling for Proust than for Flaubert, for Faulkner than for Proust, for Beckett than for Faulkner. It is a question of something else from now on. . . . In the modern narrative one might say that time was cut off from its temporality. It doesn't flow any more. It isn't the agent for anything any more.' According to Nathalie Sarraute, the new novel should preserve and promote 'that element of indetermination, opacity and mystery that one's own actions always have'. The psychological element could stay on condition that it must not be converted back into character or plot. But the theory of the *nouveau roman* is more interesting than the actual fiction. In his essay 'The Novel as Research' Michel Butor defines the traditional novel as 'the novel which raises no questions'. In a world which is changing so rapidly 'new forms will reveal new things in reality, new connexions', while 'traditional narrative techniques are incapable of integrating all the new relations thus created'. Far from being antithetical to realism in the novel, formal invention is indispensable to it. If the novelist carries his realism far enough, he finds that the formal relationship he has set up between the component parts of his fiction is making a statement about external reality. The complexity of the reality he experiences will be reflected in the complexity of his structure, 'certain portions playing in relation to the whole the same part that the whole plays in relation to reality'.

But this, as Butor says, can happen only when the novelist is willing to make demands on his reader, forcing him to question his habitual ways of organizing his responses to experience. In England today the novelist is under pressure to give his reader an easy time. While television is both discouraging the reading habit and providing an alternative form of easily digestible stories for mass consumption, inflation is increasing the price of books and reducing the number of novels that publishers can afford to bring out. The 'difficult' novelist is liable to be squeezed out of the market altogether, while many are writing as if nothing mattered except to keep the reader constantly entertained.

Before the war, *avant-gardisme* went hand in hand with obscurity, but today the most obviously 'experimental' writer is not necessarily the most difficult. B. S. Johnson's concern to make his work available to a wide reading public became increasingly evident in the last novels he wrote before he killed himself in 1973. When he started to write, he was, as he said himself, 'besotted by Irish writers like Sam Beckett, James Joyce and Flann O'Brien'.[1] (Beckett thought highly of Johnson's work.) But he was only superficially affected by the *nouveau roman*. According to Roland Barthes, writing becomes real writing when it prevents the reader from answering the question 'Who is speaking?' In B. S. Johnson's work the answer is always obvious.

If Günter Grass was the first contemporary novelist to imitate the techniques of Laurence Sterne, B. S. Johnson was the first in England. Grass's *The Tin Drum* was published in 1959; the English translation was available two years later in the States and the following year in England. Johnson had studied the eighteenth-century novel when he read English at London University during the late fifties, and in 1963 he published his first novel, *Travelling People*, which was amusingly full of Sterne-like typographical tricks and Sterne-like digressions.

[1] 'Fat Man on a Beach' in *Beyond the Words*, edited by Giles Gordon, London, 1975.

B. S. Johnson

His second book, *Albert Angelo* (1964), is about a young architect who has to work as a supply teacher.[1] Not content with such devices as printing dialogue and inner monologue in separate columns and having holes cut into the pages for the reader to see what is coming, Johnson interrupts himself three quarters of the way through his narrative with the explosive explication that he is really talking about himself and about writing. The fiction is a lying stratagem. He had abandoned the girl who, in the story, abandons his hero.

The third novel, *Trawl* (1966) is more Beckettian in manner, but the syntax is simpler, the descriptions of sexual encounters more entertaining, and the strategy of the relationship between the narrative 'I' and the autobiographical 'I' less sophisticated. Again Johnson is focusing on his own experience, as if it would be dishonest to attempt anything else. As he said in 1967 in an interview on the radio:[2]

> I'm certainly not interested in the slightest in writing fiction. Where the difficulty comes in is that 'novel' and 'fiction' are not synonymous. Certainly I write autobiography, and I write it in the form of a novel. What I don't write is fiction.

To read a newspaper or to switch from one television programme to another is to form a multiple impression of disconnected narratives. *The*

[1] A teacher employed on a short notice basis to meet special demands created by absence of regular staff.

[2] Quoted in Bernard Bergonzi, *The Situation of the Novel*, London, 1970.

Unfortunates (1969) was presented in twenty-seven unbound sections. The reader is told which is the first and which is the last, but he can read the rest in any order, sharing something of the writer's uncertainty about how to organize material which is necessarily autobiographical. The voice and the experience are both B. S. Johnson's. *The Unfortunates* was followed in 1971 by *House Mother Normal*, which he described as 'a geriatric comedy'. It consists of nine interior monologues each of which occupies nine pages. Blank pages represent moments of blank-mindedness. The inmates of an old people's home are playing games. Certain events come clearly into focus, as when 'Pass the parcel' culminates in unwrapping a piece of dog-shit, but it is sometimes hard to construe the first eight monologues until their meaning is clinched by the ninth, which comes from the House Mother, a divorced woman of forty-two. Her motive for coupling with the dog is apparently that she wants the inmates to feel disgusted with something other than their own bodies.

The next novel, *Christie Malry's Own Double-Entry* (1973) is about an intractable bank clerk, who not only acts on the assumption that society is in his debt, but opens a double-entry account to keep records. He decides on the cash value of each aggravation and each pleasure, but the debit entries always exceed the credits, and the only way he finds of working towards balancing the ledger is by taking increasingly drastic action against society. The chapter headings and the chatty asides to the reader are reminiscent of Fielding and Sterne, while the matter-of-factness in the account of poisoning a reservoir with cyanide and causing the death of 20,479 innocent West Londoners recalls Robbe-Grillet's deadpan prose in his outline for the perfect crime in *Project for a Revolution in New York* (1970).

Johnson's last novel before his suicide reverts to veracity. *See the Old Lady Decently* (1975) is the first part of a trilogy—*The Matrix Trilogy*—centred on his mother, who died of cancer in 1971. 'The debt one owes to one's parents, which I had thought one paid by having children oneself, I now see is more nearly paid by having to watch the mother die.' Her cancer becomes symbolical of the mother country's decay over the last forty years. Not knowing the facts in detail, he had to invent episodes for the restaurant kitchen where she worked, but he tried to compensate for the fiction by interpolating factual descriptions of himself concocting it, glad to be interrupted by his children. The narrative is also interrupted with photographic reproductions of documents, letters and concrete poems, including two in the shape of a female breast. The novel ends with a punning Joycean celebration of his own pre-natal life, an embryo inside Emily.

Ann Quin was another experimentalist whose career ended in suicide. Her first novel, *Berg* (1964) was disturbingly vivid and outstandingly well written, despite the borrowings from Beckett and Sarraute, who infected Ann Quin with her idiosyncratic disdain for inverted commas. Dialogue rubs shoulders with unspoken thoughts in this compulsive impersonation of a forty-year-old man compulsively spying on his father's squalid affair in a seaside hotel.

Ann Quin's obsessive theme was triangular relationships involving a couple and an outsider. Berg steals his father's mistress, intending to kill the old man. In *Three* (1966) Ann Quin prefigured her own death by drowning. It is a story about a girl who goes off in a rowing-boat, leaving behind a suicide note, diaries and tape-recordings. She has been obsessed by the intimacy between Leonard and Ruth; the idea of death is a weapon to make them obsessed with her. What fails is the attempt to translate free-association into very loose blank verse.

In *Passages* (1969) the couple feels incomplete without the third partner. Against an unparticularized Greek background, a girl is searching for her brother, who is either dead or perhaps just displaced, like other displaced persons; her lover is less clearly focused. The blurb says he is a masculine reflection of her, in search of himself. As in *Three*, some of the best and most economical writing takes the form of extracts from the girl's diaries, but Ann Quin resembled B. S. Johnson in wanting to include herself in the story, and some of the marginal notes in small print reveal too much of the personal fantasies behind the diary entries.

The last novel she completed, *Tripticks* (1972) satirizes the American way of life—bitterly, but not very successfully. She also fails to adapt stylistically to the cartoon-strip illustrations provided by Carol Annand. The novel Ann Quin failed to complete, *The Unmapped Country*, might have been very good indeed.[1] It is reminiscent of Sylvia Plath's *The Bell Jar* not only in subject-matter but in intensity, while the interpolation of diary entries and conversations suggests that this method might have been developed very interestingly.

[1] Twenty-two pages of it are published in Giles Gordon's *Beyond the Words*, 1975.

With *The Ghost of Henry James* (1970) the thirty-year-old David Plante made one of the most promising novelistic débuts so far seen in the seventies. A good deal of the book's resonance depends on its title, which is, however, vindicated. The narrative poses the question of whether a Jamesian novel can still be written and answers it with delicate ambiguity. These young people might be grandchildren of Henry James's characters. Rich enough to devote their time wholly to personal relationships, articulate, sophisticated, well connected, highly bred, they move with an innate capacity for irony between New England, London, Rome and Tuscany, sometimes staying at the same kind of decaying nineteenth-century hotels as their fictional ancestors, poised with the same elegant, listless, wordy uncertainty between past and future.

Four brothers and a sister, they are un-Jamesian both in the casual speed at which they become homosexually or heterosexually entangled with other people and then disentangled. Nothing lasts except their involvement with each other, and even this changes in quality when Henry dies. Their existence seems to belong to his ghost, as to that of the other Henry. It is as if their self-consciously literary language is mocking them for being unable to escape onto a lower level.

David Plante's next three novels, *Slides* (1971), *Relatives* (1972) and *The Darkness of the Body* (1974) do not fulfil the promise of his first. Taking *The Marble Faun* as its point of departure, *Slides* failed to establish the same kind of richly suggestive relationship with Nathaniel Hawthorne as its predecessor had with Henry James. The similarities with *The Ghost of Henry James* are deliberate, almost ostentatious: it is another story about five rich adolescents who depend emotionally on each other's short-circuitings as they weave their leisurely love-lives between Boston and Rome. Though they are not related this time, their coupling seems scarcely less incestuous. And the narrative is fragmented into the same number of brief chapters—sixty-seven.

Relatives has only three characters at the centre of it, but instead of bringing them into clearer focus, the narrowing of the pattern makes it more worrying that so much is left unexplained. The abstentions—from judging, from developing character or situation—now appear to derive from self-indulgence rather than from self-discipline. *The Darkness of the Body* is intermittently reminiscent of Ann Quin. A homosexual turns heterosexual to displace the male half of a couple; and part of the action is set against an indefinitely Greek background.

Christine Brooke-Rose is the novelist who has been most directly influenced by the *nouveau roman*. Her first book *Languages of Love* (1957) was a fairly straightforward story of London University students, espresso bars and a love affair between a married lecturer and a woman on the brink of conversion to Catholicism. *The Dear Deceit* (1960) told its story backwards, starting from the death of a reprehensible pornographer, and pushing progressively and analytically towards childhood. *The Middlemen* (1961) is about an affair between a public relations officer and a psychotherapist whose lives are surrounded by the go-betweens of the communications industry.

The watershed in Christine Brooke-Rose's development came in 1964 with *Out*, which presents the aftermath of a nuclear holocaust. The configuration of the earth has been altered, and current racial roles have been reversed: the colourless man is subservient to the coloured. But the novel's style is even more striking than its substance—the narrative is weighed down with slow-moving quasi-scientific descriptions of physical realities. The debt to Robbe-Grillet is obvious, as it is in *Such* (1966) which is like *The Dear Deceit* in making death into a starting-point. After undergoing an operation, the central character has been dead for three days before the deliberately confused and confusing narrative—it moves like a jazz improvisation—plots the resurrection of his intellect, laboriously reassembling its scattered components.

Between (1968) is livelier. A girl who does simultaneous translations, the heroine is constantly between two languages. She is also between youth and middle-age and between two jobs. As she flies from one international conference to another, phrases and languages interrupt each other in her consciousness, forming word-clusters which are often funny, sometimes beautiful. There's not much action, but the jostling of remembered dialogues and situations is quite dramatic.

Seven years elapsed before the publication of the next novel, *Thru* (1975). Christine Brooke-Rose had been lecturing in Vincennes, and questions raised by French Structuralists about the nature of a text are reflected and refracted in the highly-wrought text of *Thru*, which teases the reader with a series of typographical truth-games. Arguments about linguistic analysis, verbal and visual variations on the theme of mirror images, concrete poems, fragments of a love story, lists, diagrams and facsimiles of hand-written texts compete for space on the page, but the reader has to work very hard to form his own patterns out of the author's.

One of the few novelists who can rival her intellectual agility is Brigid Brophy, whose *In Transit* (1969) has more than polyglot word-play in common with *Between*. Brigid Brophy's narrator is liable first to forget his (or her) sex and later to alternate between the two, sometimes splitting the text into columns so as to separate the male and female alternatives. With its multi-language announcements over loudspeakers, an airport provides a paradigm of depersonalized internationalism. There is also a television parlour game in which the panel guesses at the guest's perversion, and the games Brigid Brophy plays with the reader include the fabrication of an opera to the title *Alitalia*.

The plays of Harold Pinter have had less influence on fiction than might have been expected. Many novelists have abdicated in the same way from godlike knowingness, but few have profited from his technique of discovering dramatic potentialities in the fallibility of memory and the impossibility of making any accurate statement about past events. Gabriel Josipovici, who is also a playwright, has written the fiction which most invites comparison with Pinter's drama. The starting point for *Inventory* (1968) was the word that became its title. The idea of listing random objects and the idea of inventing combined to generate a fiction about Joe, who is inventorying the contents of a flat once occupied by two men, one of whom killed himself. A girl named Susan seems to have been partly responsible for the suicide. But the events cannot be reconstructed objectively from the clues provided by objects in the flat and by her words.

Words (1971) also has a Pinteresque atmosphere, though the usual Pinter triangle has been elaborated into a pentagon. A mysterious battle for power is fought within five points formed by two couples, both liable to break up, and one of the husbands' ex-girlfriend, who is liable to elope with him. The narrative of *The Present* (1975) oscillates between three viewpoints, which provide contradictory versions of the same triangular relationship between a couple and a lodger, but it is not even certain who is the husband and who is the lodger, whether they are living in a London flat or in the country or whether there are children. Again the title is significant. We are puzzled about whether we are in the present tense, the past or a fantasy about the future. Most of the novel is written in dialogue which, unlike David Plante's, is flat, down-to-earth, naturalistic. This increases the deadliness of the implicit threat to the novel's traditional criteria. Can truth to individual experience possibly be enough when three versions of a story can be presented in such a way that each invalidates the other two?

2

Not landlocked in insularity

IRIS MURDOCH JOHN FOWLES DORIS LESSING

Deprived of novelty, the novel ceases to be itself, but the most important innovations are not necessarily the formal inventions which disrupt either the syntax or the arrangement of print on the page. To categorize novelists as either experimental or traditional is as simplistic as to treat realism and experiment as mutually exclusive, and it is hardly less misleading to discuss contemporary fiction as if there are three main types: American, French and English. American novelists are usually characterized as energetic and uninhibited romantic mythologists, free-ranging in fantasy, free-wheeling in form; the French are assumed to be obsessed with the formal problems which are ignored by the English novelists, who carry on in their insular way as if the nineteenth century weren't quite over yet. Admittedly, some of our novelists have been trying so hard to please a middle-brow public and reacting so hard against the *avant-gardisme* of James Joyce and Virginia Woolf that they have reverted to the narrative methods of Arnold Bennett and H. G. Wells. Still, between the extremes of retrogression and the extremes of experimentalism, there is a great variety of possibilities.

The fiction which has probably been most influential of all in the post-war period has been produced outside the three main national camps: by Borges, Beckett and Nabokov. None of these is committed to the idea of the novel. 'Why take five hundred pages,' asks Borges, 'to develop an idea whose oral demonstration fits into a few minutes?' His fastidious short stories are like exquisite crystals precipitated out of the *mélange* in his consciousness of literature, images and ideas. Since 1960 when Beckett published *How It Is*, his fictions have all been brief, fragmentary, un-novelistic, while Nabokov's two best novels, *Lolita* (1955) and *Pale Fire* (1962) are both disguised as non-fiction, the first perfunctorily, the second elaborately. In all three writers, realistic landscape disappears as words tend increasingly to become objects in their own right and the author's power to form patterns with them becomes symbolical of the relationship between the individual and the environment. Solipsism may be a danger, but abstraction seems to offer the best refuge from the chaos of contingency.

Looser and more empirical than the French novel, more ambitous and less personal than the English, the American novel was quick to respond to these tendencies. Naturalism had never got a grip on it. Melville and Hawthorne wrote fables. Dreiser and Steinbeck, heavyweight champions of naturalism, fought on a lower literary level. If Lukacs was right to identify the drift towards allegory as the main current in European modernism from Kafka to Beckett, the American novel was floating with the tide. The English novel seemed to be moving much more slowly, but I want to argue that far from being disadvantageous, its ballast of naturalism has helped it towards the kind of realism that Butor desiderated.

The scene is still cluttered with enough old-fashioned novels to give some plausibility to the view that we are landlocked in insularity, separated from the mainstream of post-symbolist myth-making. It is certainly true that we have no counterparts to the Americans Thomas Pynchon and John Barth, but the best work of Iris Murdoch, John Fowles and Doris Lessing is strongly anti-traditional, though it also has deep roots in the nineteenth-century novel.

Iris Murdoch's *Under the Net* (1954) was written under the influence of Sartre, Beckett and Raymond Queneau. In 1968, the year in which she published *The Nice and the Good*, she was saying that the writer to whom she owed most was Shakespeare. 'It's his extraordinary ability to combine a marvellous pattern or myth with the expansion of the characters as absolutely free persons, independent of each other.' At this time she was not conscious of any desire to experiment. In the same interview[1] she said 'I feel myself that the *élan* of the great nineteenth-century novel isn't spent, that there's plenty of room for people to go on trying to write like Tolstoy or Dickens or Jane Austen, just doing it in the modern idiom, without any question of modernity coming in at all.' But she seems to have been influenced less by the narrative style of the great nineteenth-century novelists than by the Shakespearean elements in their work, the power of structuring, the cumulatively suggestive effect of rhythms, the grouping of characters into patterns in accordance with an invisible grid of moral criteria, the clusters of images that take on increasing symbolic significance as they grow inextricably into the tangle of plot.

Trained as a philosopher, Iris Murdoch went on teaching philosophy throughout the sixties. Born in 1919, she began writing at the beginning

[1] With Ronald Bryden, *The Listener*, 4 April 1968.

Iris Murdoch

of the war and she had completed five novels before she started on *Under the Net*, the first she published. Her fiction seems to have been motivated partly by a fear that words, concepts, theories increase one's distance from physical things and experiences. There may even have been an element of wanting to compensate or do penance for her philosophizing. The hero of *Under the Net* is a word man, a translator, who argues against the view (represented by a man of action) that 'all theorizing is flight. We must be ruled by the situation itself and this is unutterably particular. Indeed it is something to which we can never get close enough, however hard we may try, as it were, to crawl under the net.'

Iris Murdoch's fiction distils and dramatizes her own ambivalence on this question, and in a philosophical essay published in 1959, 'The Sublime and the Beautiful Revisited',[1] she argued 'Contingency must be defended, for it is the essence of personality. And here is where it becomes important to remember that a novel is written in words, to remember that "eloquence of suggestion and rhythm" of which James spoke. A novel must be a house fit for free characters to live in; and to combine form with respect for reality with all its contingent ways is the highest art of prose.' But has she allowed her own characters enough autonomy to become realistic? The uncertainty has plagued her. Without resorting to mimicry, for which she

[1] *Yale Review*, XLIX, 1959.

has only a limited talent, she has tried, as she told Frank Kermode,[1] to create 'a lot of people who are not me . . . Yet often it turns out in the end that something about the structure of the work itself, the myth as it were of the work, has drawn all these people into a sort of spiral, or into a kind of form which ultimately is the form of one's own mind.' This happens in her most Beckettian novel, *Bruno's Dream* (1969), which centres on the contracting consciousness of a very old man, very slowly dying, surrounded by possessions. But the Indian deities, Shiva and Parvati, polarize the other characters strongly, and the sexual differentiation is the only one to survive clearly.

The theme of manipulation had occurred in earlier novels: in *A Fairly Honourable Defeat* (1970), by focusing on a man who regards other people as puppets, she makes a fresh attempt to master her own tendency to abuse her power of manipulation.

One of her weaknesses as a novelist is her inclination to assume that a problem can be solved by incorporating a disguised reference to it. The very accident-proneness of the central character in *An Accidental Man* (1971) looks like a hopeful gesture in the direction of contingency, and it is not enough to make someone tell someone else 'You don't know what real people smell like'; she needs to demonstrate that she does.

The Black Prince, published in 1973, is the best novel she has yet written. It is also the most ingeniously structured and the most experimental. The thriller-like action, which involves murder, is ironically set in a complex series of frames—a method comparable to Nabokov's. There are two Forewords, one by the imaginary editor, the other by the imaginary author, and there are six Postscripts, one by the author, four by characters, one by the editor. By offering multiple interpretations of the main events, Iris Murdoch hardens the core of apparent actuality at the same time as puncturing the authority of any narrator, including herself. The version of the 'truth' that emerges from the proceedings of the law-court is very different from the resultant 'truth' that emerges from the novel, but Miss Murdoch makes its incompleteness into a virtue.

The Sacred and Profane Love Machine (1974) is unusual in equipping the characters with a self-awareness which is a distinctive element in their personalities. ('We live in dream worlds,' says Montague Small, a high-brow thriller-writer.) Like the *nouveau roman* authors, Iris Murdoch is

[1] Interview in *Partisan Review*, Spring 1963.

John Fowles

providing ornate metaphors for the process of literary creation, but instead of thinning the life-blood of actuality, she is increasing the tension and—intermittently at least—heightening the vividness. Like David Plante and Christine Brooke-Rose, she is writing fiction which is also literary criticism. Her seventeenth novel, *A Word Child* (1975), is least convincing when the narrator is summarizing the experiences that fixated him on words; he is at his best when she is playing games with our awareness that his character could disintegrate into the words she is feeding to us through his mouth.

Like Iris Murdoch, John Fowles is a fabulator in Robert Scholes's sense of the word[1]. The fabulator takes particular pleasure in design, being less concerned with the representation of reality than with the construction of a verbal artefact that will please and stimulate the reader. Ideas and ideals become more important than objects or actions. Comedy and irony at once signal the writer's awareness of his own limitations and license him to embark on absurdly ambitious schemes. John Fowles's second novel, *The Magus* (1966) is like a Borges short story blown up to the size of a modern monster which can try to swallow the whole of classical mythology. *The French Lieutenant's Woman* (1969) is a novel which contains an elaborate piece of literary criticism. Set in Victorian Lyme Regis, it is written for the most part like a Victorian novel, lovingly ornamented with circumlocutions to recreate the authentic flavour of the language that was then

[1] *The Fabulators*, London, 1967.

spoken and written. But Fowles keeps cutting holes in the fabric of his pastiche with a reference to Marshall McLuhan or a jokey parenthesis in a conventionally worded sentence:

> Later that night Sarah might have been seen—though I cannot think by whom, unless a passing owl—standing at the open window of her unlit bedroom.

Then on page ninety-seven he halts the narrative (almost like B. S. Johnson in *Albert Angelo*) to say that 'in the age of Alain Robbe-Grillet and Roland Barthes' he has been writing in 'a convention universally accepted at the time of my story: that the novelist stands next to God. He may not know all, yet he tries to pretend that he does.' But Fowles climbs back on the narrative tightrope, resuming the chatty asides which work like Brechtian alienation effects, while in the final chapter he introduces himself as impresario to offer the reader alternative endings.

None of these tricks dissipates the emotional force of the effects he has brought off, while still working within the limitations of his Victorian manner. But he is doing more than expressing his own ambivalence towards the period and the form. He is measuring them against what has replaced them.

Fowles read French at Oxford and he has said[1] that he was 'brought up really in a French tradition of literature'. He made one attempt at a fiction in the style of the *nouveau roman* but abandoned it. His familiarity with contemporary French writing may have made him nervously conscious of himself as a string-pulling novelist, but in *The French Lieutenant's Woman*, as in *The Magus*, he turns the self-consciousness very skilfully to advantage.

Doris Lessing's roots in nineteenth-century fiction are no less deep for her having been born in Persia and brought up in Rhodesia. 'For me,' she wrote in 1957,[2] 'the highest point of literature was the novel of the nineteenth century, the work of Tolstoy, Stendhal, Dostoevsky, Balzac, Turgenev, Chekhov; the work of the great realists.' She re-read their books continuously, she said. In her preface to the 1972 edition of *The Golden Notebook*, which first came out in 1962, she wrote that her intention had been to follow the great European novelists of the nineteenth century 'in describing the intellectual and moral climate of our mid-century'. This is certainly one of the principal objectives in her novel-cycle *Children of*

[1] In an interview with Lorna Sage in *The New Review*, Vol. I, No. 7.
[2] In *Declaration*, edited by Tom Maschler. London, 1957.

Violence, which she started at the beginning of the fifties and finished towards the end of the sixties. The first four volumes are devoted to the African scene and to the experience of growing up within a white settlers' enclave. What she wrote in the first volume, *Martha Quest* (1952), about her heroine is arguably true of herself:

> She was adolescent, and therefore bound to be unhappy; British, and therefore uneasy and defensive; in the fourth decade of the twentieth century, and therefore inescapably beset with problems of race and class; female, and obliged to repudiate the shackled women of the past.

She has described the cycle of novels as a *Bildungsroman*, but the final volume, *The Four-Gated City* (1969), moves off in a different direction. The action shifts to London, Martha's own life ceases to be central and an apocalyptic coda prophetically visualizes a new breed of children, survivors of a nuclear holocaust, who are equipped with finer sensibilities.

Briefing for a Descent Into Hell (1971) breaks even further away from naturalism. Like Ronald Laing, she refuses to discriminate against 'insanity' with the assumption that 'delusions' have no information content that is relevant to 'objective reality'. A classics professor is admitted to hospital believing that he has been wrecked in the mid-Atlantic, and the narrative 'cuts' between letters, medical reports and his stream of consciousness while he identifies with Sinbad and Ulysses, as his sanity is jeopardized by drugs and shock therapy. Doris Lessing had never before given her imagination such a free rein nor (except in her best short stories) kept her prose on a tighter rein.

The Summer Before the Dark (1973) is more conventionally written except in the sequences describing a recurring dream about carrying a dying seal towards an unreachable sea. In these the prose reaches back towards archetypal images. One has the feeling that she would have preferred to suggest them wordlessly. The drive behind the novel is strongly reductionist, and the first half is not so good as the second, when words and storyline are stripping Kate down to her rudimentary identity as a woman, testing her ability to slough off the layers of behaviour accumulated during twenty-five years of success as a middle-class wife and a mother of four children.

The next novel, *Memoirs of a Survivor* (1974), compellingly reworks the futuristic nightmare that Doris Lessing had sketched in the coda to *The*

Four-Gated City. In *The Summer Before the Dark* the dreams came as interludes; in *Memoirs of a Survivor* nightmare takes a firm grip on the whole structure, charging the prose with a new intensity.

3

A question of length

ANGUS WILSON   ANTHONY POWELL   MURIEL SPARK

When the novel was at the height of its popularity, family readings were commonplace. Father liked his own voice best, but Mother and the older children would be given their turn occasionally. I know of one television-less family where novels are still read aloud; there may be others but there cannot be many. The length of the Victorian novel was determined partly by the size of the demand for fiction and partly by methods of publication. Dickens and Hardy did much of their best work for monthly serialization, committing themselves irrevocably to a beginning without knowing quite how they would write the next twenty-three instalments or how they would tie the threads of plot neatly together in the last. The modern novelist, who can revise his beginning after writing his ending, is usually wise to reduce substance in the process of refining it. Narrative economy is encouraged both by publishers, who have to meet the rising costs of printing and paper, and by the habits of the public, which has more choices than ever before in the history of leisure and which, on the whole, enjoys solitary reading less than group activities like watching television *en famille* or listening to poetry in pubs.

Reviewing Angus Wilson's *As If By Magic* (1973), John Bayley complained that the very strenuousness of its efforts to be 'totally contemporary' made it look about three years out of date. Six years had elapsed since the previous novel *No Laughing Matter*: had Angus Wilson been able to publish *As If By Magic* in episodes as he wrote it, it would not only have seemed more up to date, but we could have had more enjoyment from the parts, relishing the piquant details without worrying about the problems of integration.

Unlike John Fowles, Angus Wilson feels no embarrassment about adopting 'the "God's eye view" in frequent use among the nineteenth-century novelists I admire. I was surprised to find how unfamiliar this had now become; indeed, in the United States it had to be explained as a revival (I am glad to say successful) of an archaic form.'[1] In the fifties he was hostile to experiment. Writing about the reactionary 'revival of traditional nineteenth-century forms' in the *London Magazine* (April 1954) he said 'It has told against experiments in technique and against exploration of personal sensitivity. I belong to this reaction myself and I believe that it has been a valuable one that has revitalized and restored the novel form.' But *The Old Men at the Zoo* (1961) was a departure into futurist fantasy, and neither *Late Call* (1964) nor *No Laughing Matter* (1967) were conservative in form.

It is hard to avoid the word 'Dickensian' in describing his work, but at least we should qualify it. He has spoken to Frank Kermode[2] about his attempts to choke down the strong sadistic impulses that appear in his books, not knowing whether they belong to his private personality or to the world he is describing. Ten years later, in a *Guardian* interview, he said that what he cared about in Dickens was the 'underworld of violent strains and stresses which is trying to pierce its way through'. Dickens uses rivers and fogs to represent forces that had been repressed; Angus Wilson is not at his best in his Dickensian delineation of minor characters or in his attempts on a Dickensian scale to represent slow-moving social change, but rather when—running the risk of appearing sadistic—he lets the underground forces penetrate to the surface. He also resembles Dickens (and differs from the other contemporary novelists I've been discussing) in being a superb mimic. Perhaps there is an element of sadism in all mimicry. Certainly there was in the satirical mimicry of his early short stories, and the best moments in his uneven novels are epiphanies that depend on mimicry to capture the exact quality of a moment.

If the twenty-five pages that constitute Book I of *No Laughing Matter* had been presented as a self-contained story, it would have deserved to be rated extremely highly; the material is capable of development, but the next 400-odd pages do not stay on such a high level because the gradual development of character is not Angus Wilson's *forte* and, like Doris

[1] 'The Novelist and the Narrator', *English Studies Today* (Second Series), Bern, 1961.

[2] *Partisan Review*, Spring 1963.

Lessing in *The Four-Gated City*, he is over-ambitious in trying to make one middle-class family into a microcosm for a wide range of social history.

Anthony Powell's series of twelve novels (1951–75), *A Dance to the Music of Time*, benefits from his being unworried about the width of his social gamut and from his skill in writing the whole sequence with the economy of a short story. Even when the narrative appears to be moving slowly—it becomes almost processional when it describes processions, as at Lord Erridge's funeral in *Books Do Furnish a Room* (1971) or Widmerpool's installation as Chancellor in *Hearing Secret Harmonies* (1975)—the texture is always rich in information. Yet the syntax never becomes clotted. Sometimes a single sardonic phrase, such as 'Pamela's gladiatorial sex-life during the war' combines the approximation of chatty casualness with suggestive resonance.

What keeps the narrative on a high level is the combination of expertise and relaxation in Anthony Powell's use of separate but carefully selected incidents to enrich each other. Sometimes he suggests an interpretation, as when Widmerpool congratulates the Quiggin twins on their accuracy in throwing paint at him, and Nicholas Jenkins's narrative proceeds to a comparison with Widmerpool's reaction to the assault that Barbara Goring had perpetrated forty years earlier by pouring sugar over his head. Sometimes the readers are left to pull threads together for themselves. It would be better if they could be allowed to do this more often, but one disadvantage of the narrative method is that Anthony Powell has to address himself simultaneously to readers with clear memories of the earlier novels, readers who have three-quarters forgotten them and readers who haven't read them. One advantage is that the narrative can flow as smoothly as any stream of consciousness between present, recent past, remote past and speculation about the future or about significance, but Anthony Powell preserves the air of making his points as he would in a conversation with a friend. He never assumes god-like omniscience. He spoke to Michael Frayn[1] of 'the difficulty in understanding, even remotely, why people behave as they do . . . One passes through the world knowing few, if any, of the important things about the people with whom one has been from time to time in the closest intimacy.'

Bernard Bergonzi has shrewdly suggested[2] that many of the stylistic

[1] *The Observer*, 7 September 1975.
[2] *The Situation of the Novel*, London, 1970, p. 151.

stratagems in *A Dance to the Music of Time* are attempts to cope with the reader's loss of confidence in the novelist's old-fashioned power of creation. It is also relevant, I think, that Anthony Powell has approximated as closely as a modern novelist can to the old method of serial publication, bringing out his twelve volumes at fairly regular intervals over twenty-five years. When he started writing them in the late forties he could not have known that the final episodes would revolve around student dissent in the seventies. But the books are nearly all short. Concentration has been achieved by refining.

His style has matured with Nicholas Jenkins's maturing awareness of his own behaviour patterns. Reviewing *Books Do Furnish a Room* in the *New Statesman*,[1] Philip Larkin objected that 'A formal, slightly absurd view of life requires a matching style. Mr Powell's is Comic Mandarin, a descendant of Polysyllabic Facetiousness . . . it does in fact suggest that nothing it describes should be taken quite seriously.' But it is also quite adequate to the task of presenting events that elicit a complex reaction, serious on some levels. A great deal is left out. There are things a gentleman never discusses. There are also things which aren't done, and Anthony Powell is clever at embarrassing his narrator by making his characters do them. Solecisms never come nearer to seeming soulful.

The novel that Muriel Spark set in Jerusalem, *The Mandelbaum Gate* (1965), is a sizeable book; after finishing it she decided never again to write at such length. She had been a poet and critic before she established herself as a short story writer by winning the *Observer* competition in 1951. She came to the novel only when she was commissioned to write one. *The Comforters*, her first, was published in 1957, when she was nearly forty, but then she wrote five more within four years.

Always an economical writer, she entered on a new phase of compression with *The Public Image* (1968), working with a smaller cast of characters than before, a sparser use of background detail, a narrower span of time, a stricter principle of relevance and a more aggressive irony. 'Ridicule,' she has said, 'is the only honourable weapon we have left.' In 'Muriel Spark's Fingernails', an essay to which I am indebted,[2] Malcolm Bradbury calls these novels 'end-directed'. (His title is not an allusion to the sharpness of her satirical claws but to James Joyce's god-like writer,

[1] 19 February 1971.
[2] In *Possibilities: Essays on the State of the Novel*, London, 1973.

paring his fingernails.) 'No author', he writes, 'could be surer about where things are going. From her novels the beginning, which creates expectation and freedom, and the middle, which substantiates and qualifies it, seem absent. Her people arise at the last, *from* the last, what has withered is a world of motive, purpose, aspiration. The curious inescapability of plot is her subject, in some real sense her satisfaction.' To an even greater extent than before, she is making her statement through her use of a fictional convention, working on our awareness that plotting is what a novelist does.

In *The Public Image* an intelligent film writer aims his suicide like a missile at the career of his unintelligent actress wife, whose public image has for so long been falsifying both their lives. Miss Spark is cleverly economical in her contrivance of background and foreground to illuminate one another as she moves her characters into the ambiance of a Fellini-like director in Rome, where the public relations lady manipulates the surfaces of their lives.

In *The Mandelbaum Gate* the central character dismissed the *nouveau roman* as 'repetition, boredom, despair, going nowhere for nothing, all of which conditions are enclosed in a tight unbreakable statement of the times at hand'. But *The Driver's Seat* (1970) adopts the French techniques, describing surfaces meticulously as it moves ineluctably along its course over the last few hours of a woman's life. The heroine is in her thirties and she has come south, hoping to attract the man who will finish her off. Like the novelist who is really in the driver's seat, Lise is conscious of each action, each detail, in relation to the whole; like the actress in *The Public Image* she is also aware that she is a character for the myth-making newspapers. For the first time Muriel Spark narrates in the present tense.

The blurb invites us to read *The Driver's Seat* as a Gothic horror tale; reading its successor, *Not to Disturb* (1971), we have no alternative. Rain pours out of a thundery sky, the baron's demented heir is imprisoned in a wing of the old château, Nemesis cannot be held off for long. In fact the servants are already negotiating the sale of the film rights, greedy to profit from the inescapability of plot. The gruesomeness of the coming catastrophe and the gruesomeness of Muriel Spark's basic joke are inseparable.

The Abbess of Crewe (1974), set in an upper-class abbey, has affinities with the sophisticated farce of Ronald Firbank's novels, raised however to a much higher degree of intensity. The trees are bugged, and a nun cannot even make love to a Jesuit seminarist without being recorded on videotape. The parallels with the Watergate situation are reminiscent of the analogy between the dictatorial heroine in *The Prime of Miss Jean Brodie* (1962) and the Fascist dictators of the 1930s. Peter Kemp's useful critique *Muriel Spark*[1] quotes her remark: 'Fiction to me is a kind of parable. You have got to make up your mind it's not true. Some kind of truth emerges from it but it's not fact.' He also quotes from an article on Proust which she wrote for the *Church of England Newspaper* before her conversion to Catholicism. His writing, she says, derives power from 'an acceptance of that deep irony in which we are presented with the most unlikely people, places and things as repositories of inward grace.'

4

Entertaining an audience

GRAHAM GREENE KINGSLEY AMIS

Of some novels I discussed in the first section only 1600 copies were printed; Graham Greene's *The Comedians* (1966) was quick to sell 60,000 and still goes on selling in the Penguin edition. 'I doubt', he says, 'whether the best work has ever been produced in complete independence of a public. Popular *taste* makes a thoroughly bad dictator, but the awareness of an audience is an essential discipline for an artist.' Yes, but while there is no communication without compromise, the bigger the audience the bigger the compromise. The comedian and the pop singer tell us almost nothing about what it feels like to be them; Lawrence and Joyce tell us quite a lot, at the same time as creating vivid pictures of external reality. Greene is fond of quoting Chekhov's remark about novelists: 'The best of them are realistic and paint life as it is, but because every line is permeated, as with a juice, by an awareness of a purpose, you feel, besides life as it is, also life as it ought to be, and this captivates you.'

Graham Greene is strongly possessed by this double awareness, which accounts for many of the best effects he has produced. There is always a

[1] London, 1974.

penumbra around the story, the poignant possibility of a happier alternative, even when he is writing about the sadism of the Tontons Macoute in Papa Doc's Haiti (*The Comedians*), about currency smuggling in South America under the auspices of a seventy-four-year-old lady who still has a lover, an ex-war-criminal (*Travels with My Aunt*, 1971), or about a political kidnapping near the Paraguayan border with an ex-priest among the kidnappers (*The Honorary Consul*, 1973).

Graham Greene gave his first novel an epigraph from Thomas Browne: 'There is another man within me that is angry with me.' The other man has done most of the writing, insisting on a circulation of over 50,000 and the strict subordination of mood to story. Intimidated, the outer man has made his moralizing as melodramatic as his cinematic plots, though his essays on Henry James show him to be intelligent and sensitive. Serious reflection still finds its main outlet in similes that recall W. H. Auden's description of A. E. Housman as keeping 'tears like dirty postcards in a drawer'. When Scobie in *The Heart of the Matter* (1948) looks pityingly at the childlike Helen Rolt, 'The ugliness was like handcuffs on his wrists'. As a young man Greene reacted strongly against the novels of Virginia Woolf; as a successful novelist he still felt so dependent on his large public that he had to make a secret of his ingenuity, allowing his intelligence full play only in setting puzzles that most readers wouldn't notice. His debt to Conrad, for instance, is acknowledged in *It's a Battlefield* (1934) by naming a character Conrad after a merchant navy officer who had lodged in his parents' house.

Like Graham Greene, Kingsley Amis is never less than highly readable. He started out as a brave iconoclast, an originator of the vogue for anti-intellectualism, and the comedy of *Lucky Jim* (1954) was all the richer for the deadly accuracy of the satirical sniping at cultural pretentiousness, but the later novels scatter buckshot untidily over a wide range of innocuous targets loosely associated with the higher culture: 'all those rotten old churches and museums and galleries', 'filthy Mozart', foreign travel, Chablis and Henry James. A lack of respect—sometimes genuine, sometimes affected—has been used as a means of commanding respect. Brigid Brophy was provoked into calling Amis an intellectual slob, a cultural equivalent of the teddy-boy who slashed seats.

His poetry, his book reviews, his science fiction anthologies, his *James Bond Dossier*, his ghost story *The Green Man* (1967) and his thriller *The Riverside Villas Murder* (1973) have not all been addressed to the same public as the novels *I Want It Now* (1968), *Girl, 20* (1971) and *Ending Up* (1974), but his jokey animosity towards highbrows has been accompanied fairly consistently by a determined antipathy to experiment. Like Pamela Hansford Johnson, he has blamed the *avant-garde* novelists of the thirties for the slump in fiction reading, and as a book reviewer he was able to point out 'It will have been noticeable that I am being much less nasty to the unambitious novelist than to the ambitious.' He has even declared himself[1] as an enemy of style: 'Style, a personal style, a distinguished style, usually turns out in practice to mean a highly idiosyncratic noise-level in the writing, with plenty of rumble and wow from imagery, syntax and diction: Donne, Pater, Virginia Woolf.'

I Want It Now returns to the theme of hypergamy, first exploited in *Lucky Jim*. In 'The Perils of Hypergamy', an article in the *New Statesman*,[2] Geoffrey Gorer wrote:

> In *Lucky Jim*, *That Uncertain Feeling*, *Look Back in Anger*, *Room at the Top* (to mention no others) the hero, of working-class origin, is married to, or involved in a public liaison with, a middle to upper middle-class woman and doesn't really enjoy it at all, in the long run. He thinks he is 'destroyed' by her, or would be 'destroyed' by her if he didn't return to his proper working-class environment, or both are reduced to mutual misery and recrimination. These cross-class unions, with male hypergamy, don't work out, we are told with humour and anger and passion and sentimentality; and yet it is implied, if not stated, that it is only among women of this higher social class that these bright young men can expect to find wives and mistresses.

In *That Uncertain Feeling*, Amis's second novel (1955), the librarian-hero redeems himself by turning down the job he could have got by hypergamous adultery; Ronnie Appleyard in *I Want It Now* is already a successful television interviewer when the action starts. Though he is greedy in his pursuit of sex, his ambition is to marry into extreme affluence; to be redeemed he must be nauseated by his own ideal: with success in retching distance, he marries the girl without her money.

Amis's beginnings are invariably much better than his moralizing endings, but even at the beginning the satire and the story-telling are both marred by what looks like a deliberately clumsy adherence to outmoded

[1] *The Spectator*, 6 November 1959.
[2] 4 May 1957.

methods. He writes knowingly and amusingly about the television interviewer's unfair use of his professional expertise, but the satire suddenly becomes very facile when Amis adopts a god's-eye viewpoint, going inside his character to tell us that Ronnie 'had no feeling for old people as such beyond a mild dislike' and 'would not have cared a curse if the British army were to set about reoccupying the Indian sub-continent, providing they did so without calling on him for assistance'. As in Anthony Powell, the Mandarin phrases have a distancing effect, but Amis swings between Mandarin and a frank, slangy chattiness, which helps to create an illusion of intimacy with the reader, while the meta-farcical comedy invites sympathy. The dialogue is generally better written than the intervening narrative, and impassioned abuse is generally better written than routine rudeness, especially when Amis has generated enough momentum to lift himself above his usual level of carefully calculated carelessness. When the music columnist in *Girl, 20* asks the daughter of the trendy, knighted, left-wing conductor what makes her such a howling bitch, her answer takes off into an unpunctuated modernist eloquence that Amis would never risk except inside inverted commas.

I expect it's the same thing as makes you a top-heavy red-haired four-eyes who . . . likes bloody symphonies and fugues and the first variation comes before the statement of the theme and give me a decent glass of British beer and dash it all Carruthers I don't know what young people are coming to these days and a scrounger and an old woman and a failure and a hanger-on and a prig and terrified and a shower and a brisk rub-down every morning and you can't throw yourself away on a little trollop like that Roy you must think of your wife Roy old boy old boy and I'll come along but I don't say I approve and bloody dead. Please delete the items in the above that do not apply.

This is not tape-recorder reproduction of 'the way people talk' but it's very effective, and dangerously close to James Joyce.

Focused on the consciousness of five old people in a country cottage, *Ending Up* is more serious. There are some scenes of strenuous drinking, but none of sexuality—only sour, thirty-five-year-old memories of an affair between Bernard, an ex-soldier, and Shorty, his ex-batman. Interest in language is again evidenced inside inverted commas: George, an immigrant from Central Europe and Emeritus Professor of Central European History, is suffering from nominal aphasia. Unable to find the words he wants, he talks in paraphrases. But there is little evidence of interest in form. The reader is liable to be halted in embarrassment by sentences like 'Outside the sun was shining on various items of vegetation'. Even though this is intended to represent Bernard's consciousness of it, the phrasing reminds us of the author. 'Real-life nature hardly touches me,' he once wrote[1] with no sign of regret; 'I need to see it through other eyes, those of a writer or . . . the camera's.'

At the end of *Ending Up* all five characters abruptly meet their death within a couple of hours. This device would work better if it were clearer that it is partly a comment on the convention, comparable with the Jacobean multiplication of deaths in the last sequence of Kingsley Amis's television play, *A Question about Hell.*

5

With feet in the fifties

ALAN SILLITOE DAVID STOREY

The war and its ideology produced something of an Indian summer in the long life of the middle-class hero, who could so easily climb into the cockpit of a fighter and fly up to become a national hero. With the general reaction against the heroic mode in the fifties came the birth of the working-class anti-hero, who was not always hypergamous but always virile and iconoclastic. John Wain's Charles Lumley (*Hurry On Down*, 1953), Amis's Jim Dixon (*Lucky Jim*, 1954) and Iris Murdoch's Jake Donaghue (*Under the Net*, 1954) were bracketed together before John Osborne's play *Look Back in Anger* prompted the catchphrase 'angry young man'. Misleading though it was, it went on being applied to characters of the sort that emerged in a number of novels: John Braine's *Room at the Top* (1957), Alan Sillitoe's *Saturday Night and Sunday Morning* (1958), Keith Waterhouse's *Billy Liar* (1959), Stan Barstow's *A Kind of Loving* (1960) and David Storey's *This Sporting Life* (1960). Little formal innovation was involved in pioneering the literature of lower middle-class or working-class

[1] *Radio Times*, 19 September 1974.

city life, and the novelists had no more in common than the poets (including Amis, Wain, Larkin and Enright) who were grouped together in Robert Conquest's anthology *New Lines* as representatives of 'The Movement'.

Alan Sillitoe made a big impact with his Arthur Seaton, a lathe operator who sleeps with two married sisters, one of whom, a woman of forty, tries to abort herself in a hot bath. But the virile, fist-happy, beer-swilling hero produced diminishing returns as he kept recurring in Sillitoe's subsequent novels. As Frank Kermode said,[1] discussing *The Death of William Posters* (1965): 'Sillitoe's style is one of habitual violence, a deliberate reflection of the hated, cheated prole, crossed by a certain awkward artifice, which is correlative with the hero's self-education.' The writing is erratic, sometimes thin in texture, sometimes meretriciously rich. The book that puts Sillitoe's style most honestly to the test is *Raw Material* (1972), which oscillates between fiction and autobiography. His mind and his prose are both too blunt for the long sequences of free-wheeling self-examination, but the stubborn honesty is admirable and some of the characters loom up out of foggy recollection with startling vividness. After this it was disappointing to find that *The Flame of Life*, which he started in 1967 and finished in 1974, was convincing neither as a piece of fiction nor as an attempt to write honestly.

In *Radcliffe* (1963) David Storey made one of the strongest contemporary bids for greatness. The most Dostoevskian of his five novels, it is the most imperfect and the most interesting, distilling the love-hate relationship between the classes into a homosexual affair between a frail, sensitive, spiritual, Myshkin-like aristocrat and a strong-willed, robustly physical workman. In spite of reaching out so ambitiously for significance, Storey gives his violence a resonance that Sillitoe's violence lacks, but the only two novels Storey had published since *Radcliffe*—*Pasmore* (1972) and *A Temporary Life* (1973)—are both limited by their refusal to reach out.

Most of *Pasmore* had been written about 1964 as part of a *magnum opus* on which Storey had spent over seven years. Just as his play *The Contractor* is siphoned off from *Radcliffe* (using some of the same characters and the same firm of tent-contractors) so is *Pasmore* distilled from the bigger novel. It is a laconically tight-lipped account of a breakdown in a marriage, with the narrative itself flattened by a combination of depression and detachment which is best described in words spoken by Radcliffe: 'It's as

[1] *Continuities*, London, 1968.

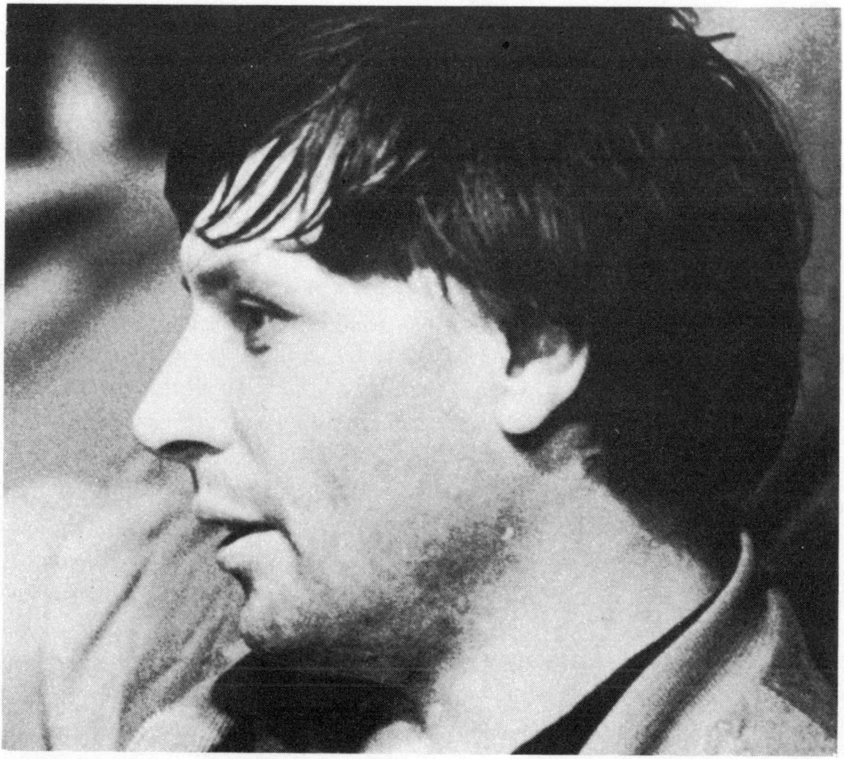

David Storey

if I don't really take part in my depression. As though, because I can watch my feelings, that somehow, they're valueless . . . synthetic, put on. Though I know they're not . . . It's hellish. Hellish . . . watching your own suffering to such an extent that you begin to suspect that it's not really suffering at all.'

Pasmore is most impressive in its low-pressure zones, such as the non-committal account of having sex with a non-committal married woman. *A Temporary Life* is too much like a draft for one of Storey's plays—in fact *Life Class* was later siphoned out of it. Unlike his plays, his previous novels had all been written very slowly. In *A Temporary Life* there is some careful descriptive writing, but the dialogue is thinly textured and sometimes contrived for comic effect, as in the over-extended sequence with the head of the local art college, whose dinner-guests have to put up with his extreme meanness and his grotesque diet.

6

The weariness of the long-distance novelist

WILLIAM GOLDING LAWRENCE DURRELL RICHARD HUGHES

One of the human needs that is not satisfied by the contemporary novel is one which had previously been met in different ways by the Book of Genesis, by classical myths of Arcadia, by pastoral poetry and by descriptions of landscape in nineteenth-century fiction. In all these the underlying assumptions are that Nature corresponds to human nature and that everything has a relationship with everything else. There was little description of the natural environment in Homer, Virgil, Chaucer or the eighteenth-century novel; whether Necessity, Fate, God or Nature was in command, human action could not but be subservient to *force majeure*. In Tolstoy, Melville, George Eliot, Zola and Hardy, nature is a powerful force, but one which can be fought. In the middle of the nineteenth century, when the rage for description was at its height, materialism was overtaking transcendentalism, and the novel was beginning to look like a scientific instrument for scrutinizing human data in relation to the environment. As in a portrait painting, wallpaper and possessions may be as relevant to characterization as clothes and complexion.

Like other believers in Original Sin, William Golding takes it for granted that generalizations can be made about human nature. The myth of all his books is, as Frank Kermode has said,[1] 'the Fall of Man, the expulsion from Paradise, erected wit and infected will'. Some of Golding's best writing is to be found in his descriptions of natural scenery. In *The Inheritors* (1955) Neanderthal Man is conquered by *homo sapiens*, with his superior capacity for control over the environment; in *Pincher Martin* (1956) the Everyman figure is alone with his memories and the sea. Since Golding's sixth novel, *The Pyramid* (1967), the only fiction he has published is *The Scorpion God* (1971) which contains three stories, one of which dates back to 1956. With its primitive setting and its confrontation between two attitudes, one more advanced than the other, the title story is reminiscent of *The Inheritors*, but inferior in its landscape painting, less convincing in

[1] In *Continuities*, op. cit.

William Golding

its representation of primitive dialogue and more awkward in its assumption of god-like insight into the characters. The second story 'Clonk Clonk' also has a primitive setting.

Reputations tarnish very quickly in a period of over-exposure, and it is already hard to remember how highly Lawrence Durrell was rated in the early sixties after completing his *Alexandria Quartet*. Pursewarden, the novelist within the novel, compares Justine to the city: 'they both have a strong flavour without having any real character.' Without justifying Durrell's wordiness, the strong flavour of Alexandria often distracted from it, but in *Tunc* (1968) and its sequel *Nunquam* (1970), the greenhouse in which he forces his language is unsuitable for his Gothic science fiction. *Monsieur or the Prince of Darkness* (1974) is a disappointing exercise in fabulation. The conjuror has overwritten his patter and the rabbit is dead long before he pulls it out of the hat.

After publishing *A High Wind in Jamaica* (1929) and *In Hazard* (1938) Richard Hughes produced nothing until 1961, when critics greeted *A Fox in the Attic* with words like 'magnificent' and 'genius'. It was announced as the first instalment of *The Human Predicament*, which was to be not a trilogy or tetralogy but a single continuous novel. The next part, *The Wooden Shepherdess*, did not appear until 1973, when Richard Hughes was seventy-two. Introducing Hitler as a character, rather in the way that Solzhenitsyn brought Stalin into *The First Circle*, *The Wooden Shepherdess* reconstructs the 1934 'night of the long knives'. Intrinsically fascinating, the historical and autobiographical elements in the novel tend to detach themselves from the fictional elements. Organization is not Richard Hughes's *forte* and even if he eventually succeeds in completing his novel, it seems very unlikely that he will be able to integrate its components.

7

In a strange land

E. M. FORSTER FRANK TUOHY THOMAS HINDE RUTH PRAWER JHABVALA FRANCIS KING OLIVIA MANNING J. G. FARRELL

A great novelist is likely to be at his best in writing about the society he was born in. Conrad was exceptional. Lawrence's Mexican and Australian novels are among his worst, while Henry James, the patrician of expatriate writers, did most of his best work between 1878 and 1886—after he had left America but before he had forgotten it. He implored Edith Wharton not to repeat his mistake: 'She must be tethered in native pastures.'

There are also novelists—important, if not great—who cannot manage so well without an unfamiliar backcloth when tensions between internal and external forces are to be dramatized. Between the two world wars, Virginia Woolf seemed to be more in touch with the modernist spirit than E. M. Forster, but post-war novelists have found her story-telling technique, which sucks everything into a stream of mental events, less useful than the more straightforward technique of Forster. His two visits to Europe (October 1901–September 1902 and March–August 1903) provided both the stimulus and the material for *Where Angels Fear to Tread* (1905) and *A Room with a View* (1908), both of which pivot on conflict between Italian emotionality and English gentility. Like these two novels, *The Longest Journey* (1907) and *Howard's End* (1910) are flawed by the assumption that everything can be measured in terms of personal relationships, but after two visits to India (in 1912 and 1921) Forster published his most penetrating novel, *A Passage to India* (1924), which centres on the failure of a loving friendship between an Englishman and an Indian to survive across the gulf created by civic inequalities based on racial prejudice and imperial exploitation, by temperamental disparities and by all the cultural and climatic differences between England and India.

We had to wait till 1971 for the publication of his homosexual novel *Maurice*, which had been written in 1913–14 and revised three times—in 1919, 1932 and 1959–60. *The Life to Come* (1972) was a collection of 14 homosexual stories, only two of which had been published previously. They had been written between 1903 and 1958; he had gone on revising some of them till 1962. The three best stories, 'Dr Woolacott', the title story and 'The Other Boat' are very much better than the novel. 'Dr Woolacott' is curiously reminiscent of Thomas Mann's *Death in Venice*, associating the alluring young male with terminal illness in a narrative channelled through a consciousness subject to illusion. The other two are about inter-racial love, and they both end in the deaths of both lovers. The novel tells the story of a suburban stockbroker whose doctor fails to hypnotize him back to 'normality'. From an unhappy relationship with a stuffy young squire, the friend of a character based on Lytton Strachey, Maurice falls in love with an uninhibited gamekeeper and the ending is sentimental but happy.

There are some extracts from Forster's diaries in Oliver Stallybrass's useful Introduction to *The Life to Come*.

> Having sat for an hour in vain trying to write a play, will analyse causes of my sterility . . . 2. Weariness of the only subject that I both can and may treat—the love of men for women and vice versa. *16 June 1911.*
>
> I should have been a more famous writer if I had written or rather published more, but sex has prevented the latter. *31 December 1965.*

In a personal memorandum of 1935 he wrote 'I want to love a strong young man of the lower classes and be loved by him and even hurt by him. That is my ticket, and then I have wanted to write respectable novels.'

The new books illuminate the mystery of his sterility between 1924 and his death in 1970: it was only in *A Passage to India* that Forster found a satisfactory means of treating the subject that really concerned him. 'Love' is the only word for the deep mutual understanding that exists between Aziz and Fielding, but thanks to the cultural and racial contrasts, intimacy can be divorced from sexuality.

Obviously I do not want to make allegations of homosexuality against all the novelists who have followed profitably in Forster's intercontinental footsteps, but it is noticeable that there are many who are not at their best in dramatizing sexual confrontations and are at their best when they can set their action a long way from home, enmeshing an Englishman in conflicts that involve contrasts of culture, race and national character.

Frank Tuohy—who has not published any novels since his two about Brazil, *The Animal Game* (1957) and *The Warm Nights of January* (1960) and his one about Poland, *The Ice Saints* (1964)—is not alone in feeling dependent on an unfamiliar environment. 'Most of what I write seems to start off with the interaction between two cultures, modes of behaviour, ways of living, etc. Sometimes this confrontation is between a foreigner and an alien environment, sometimes between groups in that environment itself. For me, the sense of displacement, loss, anxiety which happens to people derives from the world outside them, in their relationships with that world. If I thought of it as starting inside, as being a part of the self, I probably wouldn't write at all.'

It is quite a common pattern for novelists who have successfully fictionalized their foreign experiences to become less prolific and less successful when they settle down again in England. The poet D. J. Enright has published no novel since *Academic Year* (1955), which was based on his three years at the University of Alexandria. P. H. Newby's best novels *The Picnic at Sakkara* (1955) and *Revolution and Roses* (1957) have Arabian and Greek settings.

Thomas Hinde has drawn on his experiences of East Africa in *The Cage* and *A Place Like Home* (both 1962) and on his years of lecturing at American universities (1965–7 and 1969–70). His ingenious novel *High* (1968) is about an English novelist lecturing on creative writing at an American university and working simultaneously on a novel which interpenetrates not only with his experiences but with the literary effusions of people he meets—fabulation fabricated out of tales told to a traveller. In *Bird* (1970) he returns to familiar territory, with a first-person narrative that successfully impersonates a twenty-one-year-old girl who becomes involved in London's criminal underworld and enjoys being maltreated by the strong-arm man of a racketeer. *Generally a Virgin* (1972) is like *High* in being set in an American university, and *Agent* (1974) could not have been written by a man with no experience of living as a foreigner. The central character, who believes himself to be a spy in enemy territory, turns out to be a deluded psychotic in his home environment. Thomas Hinde has formidable powers of empathic mimicry. In *Bird* and in *Agent* he identifies

Thomas Hinde

Ruth Prawer Jhabvala

with two viewpoints very unlike his own, but in *Our Father* (1975) he fails to solve the technical problems involved in shifting from one viewpoint to another.

No novelist has ever immersed himself more deeply in an alien environment than Ruth Prawer Jhabvala. Her parents were Jewish—Polish and German. After going to school and university in England, she was twenty-four when she married an Indian architect and settled in India, adopting Indian habits, attitudes, values and bringing up her children as Indians. For ten years she met no Europeans. Her first two novels, *To Whom She Will* (1955) and *The Nature of Passion* (1956) are entirely about Indians. *Esmond in India* (1957) introduced her first European character—he has an Indian wife—and by 1965 she had written three more novels, exploring the drama of temperamental individuals in a hierarchical society. 'Sometimes I wrote about Europeans in India, sometimes about Indians in India, sometimes about both, but always attempting to present India to myself in the hope of giving myself some kind of foothold . . . I described the Indian scene not for its own sake but for mine.'

Her fourth novel, *The Householder*, came out in 1960 and she scripted the film of it, which was directed by James Ivory. *Shakespeare Wallah* was the next of the five screenplays she has written for him. Her productivity as a novelist diminished. *Get Ready for Battle* appeared in 1962 and *A Backward Place* in 1965 but then there was a gap of seven years before the next, *A New Dominion*, which consists of short sequences, each with a title in capital letters. The Western characters are an English boy, three girls and a missionary lady; the Indians include a man of royal birth who has got himself democratically elected to Parliament, his middle-aged sister, a student and a spiritual guide. The accumulation of brief episodes involves them in a complex web of relationships. Subtly, with an appearance of effortlessness, Ruth Prawer Jhabvala reveals a great deal about private and public life in post-imperial India.

Her latest novel, *Heat and Dust*, which won the Booker Prize, may have recourse to eighteenth-century techniques, incorporating excerpts from diaries and letters into the narrative, but the idea for the construction is cinematic, evolved out of experience in the cutting-room. Two parallel stories, separated by fifty years, are interwoven. Abdicating from the omniscience she claimed in *A New Dominion*, Ruth Prawer Jhabvala identifies only with the viewpoints of the two heroines, who are both girls who develop a passion for India, a passion which culminates in bearing a child to an Indian without any certainty of whether it is the individual man that they love.

Olivia is happily married to Douglas, a blond Englishman, representative of a government that is intruding insensitively in the India of 1923, where widows are still immolating themselves to be buried with their husband's corpse. Alienated by English incomprehension and lack of respect for the Indians' rights to live and die in their own way, Olivia runs away with a Muslim princeling, attractive, charming, arrogant, dishonest and profoundly lacking in respect for other people's lives.

The narrator is the granddaughter of Douglas by his second wife. The girl's interest in Olivia's letters and diaries is acceptable enough, while her own experience is woven into a fascinating pattern of comparison and contrast with Olivia's The British Raj has disintegrated; the glamour of the Indian nobility has faded. Other things have remained the same—the heat, the dust, the injustice, the fecklessness, the cruelty, the poverty, the superstition, the charm. Could there be causal connexions between them? The form of Mrs Jhabvala's novel goes just far enough towards answering the questions it raises.

Most of Francis King's best work has roots in the more peripatetic years of his life. After growing up in India and Switzerland, he worked for the British Council, spending about twelve years in Italy, Greece, Finland, Japan and Egypt. Since 1964 he has been living mainly in Brighton and London, but like *The Custom House* (1961) and *The Japanese Umbrella* (1964), *The Waves Behind the Boat* (1967) has a Japanese setting. *The Brighton Belle* (1968) is a collection of short stories set in Brighton; *A Domestic Animal* (1970) is reminiscent of E. M. Forster's two Italian novels in its treatment of a middle-aged novelist's homosexual desire for an Italian philosopher who was once a professional footballer; *A Game of Patience* (1974) is set in the country near Maidstone during the last year of the war; *The Needle* (1975) is set in the nastiest part of Fulham. But none of these measures up to the achievement of the period that began with his Florentine novel *The Dividing Stream* (1951) and ended with his Japanese novels.

Olivia Manning's central work is her Balkan trilogy. *The Great Fortune* (1960) and *The Spoilt City* (1962) are set in Bucharest between the summer of 1939 and the German occupation; *Friends and Heroes* (1965) is set mainly in Athens. Political and military events are filtered through the consciousness of Harriet Pringle, whose husband is employed by an organization that resembles the British Council. Olivia Manning is married to R. D. Smith, a BBC drama producer who was also given a Chair in English Literature at Londonderry University. They went to Romania together just before the war started. 'I write out of experience,' she says. 'I have no fantasy.'

The Play Room (1969) is much slighter. It is about two incidents in the life of a fifteen-year-old girl, and the schoolgirl language causes some awkwardness. *The Rain Forest* (1974) is a conventional, slow-moving novel set in the Indian Ocean on an island which is still a stronghold of the British Raj. Part of the island consists of a primeval forest, impervious to snobbery and self-importance. But the background becomes neither as specific as it should have done nor as integral to the development of relationships between the characters.

J. G. Farrell opts for both geographical and historical remoteness. His fourth novel *Troubles* (1970) deals with the Irish troubles of 1919–21. Though it was written before the present Irish troubles began, his intention was 'to use this period of the past as a metaphor for today'. As he says, 'The most important things, for the very reason that they are trivial, are unsuitable for digestion by historians . . . One of the things I have tried to do in *Troubles* is to show people "undergoing" history, to use an expression of Sartre's.' In *The Siege of Krishnapur* (1973) he turned to British India in 1857, using the same technique of developing social and historical fact into significant action, giving sinister reverberations to small events. He is an interesting writer, who is still underrated, despite the Booker prize he won in 1973.

8

ANTHONY BURGESS WILLIAM TREVOR MALCOLM BRADBURY PAUL BAILEY

Anthony Burgess once wrote five novels within twelve months: *The Doctor is Sick* (published 1960), *The Worm and the Ring* (1961), *One Hand Clapping* (1961), *The Wanting Seed* (1962), and *Inside Mr Enderby* (1963). *The Wanting Seed* is the best of these, a Malthusian nightmare of a society which is in danger of famine and tries to protect itself by encouraging homosexuality and penalizing procreation. To *Inside Mr Enderby* he later wrote two sequels, *Enderby Outside* (1968) and *The Clockwork Testament* (1974).

While his energy is unabated, his inventiveness and his satirical power have never surpassed the level they achieved in 1962, when he published both *The Wanting Seed* and *A Clockwork Orange*, which has been made into an effective film. It presents a nightmarish vision of a future England where marauding gangs of teenagers are no more terrifying than the state's methods of defending its citizens against them. Alex, the principal thug, listens to Mozart while he fantasizes about rape and murder, but he also becomes the novel's principal victim when he is brainwashed into conformism. Fascinatingly, the book is written in a specially invented slang, riddled with Russian suffixes. The boys want 'to tolchock some old veck in an alley and viddy him swim in his blood'.

Without reaching the comic heights or plumbing the lavatorial depths of *Inside Mr Enderby*, *Enderby Outside* succeeds in most of its attempts to transubstantiate jokes into situations, but the character shrivels like an old balloon when *The Clockwork Testament* translates him to the University of Manhattan as Professor of English Literature and Creative Writing.

MF (1971) germinated out of Anthony Burgess's reading of Lévi-Strauss's lecture *The Scope of Anthropology*, which describes a brother-sister incest legend common to the Iroquois and Algonquin Indians. Peppering his narrative with polyglot Joycean jokes, Anthony Burgess whips the story up into a young man's exotic encounter with a foul-mouthed double and a fat sister he never knew he had.

> Take then or leave this lump of minor art
> A novel on Napolean Bonaparte

is the first anti-heroic couplet in the verse 'Epistle to the Reader' that ends *Napoleon Symphony* (1974), but the attitude is not at all one of 'take it or leave it'. The epilogue is symptomatic of a desire to forestall or divert criticism—the same desire that swings the narrative non-committally between one style and another, alternately parodying itself and indulging in yet another Joycean monologue. Napoleon is rendered with the Enderby-like afflictions of bad breath, heartburn and bladder trouble, and there are some superbly entertaining sequences. If Anthony Burgess finally fails to integrate his material or to achieve his ambition of forcing myth and history together in a shape determined by symphonic form, at least it can be said that no one could have succeeded.

William Trevor worked as a copy-writer in an advertising agency from 1960 to 1964, between publishing his first novel *A Standard of Behaviour* (1958) and his very successful second, *The Old Boys* (1964), which showed that he had a good eye for the effort and calculation that goes into playing power games, even in situations where little power can be won. *The Boarding House* followed in 1965. For *Mrs Eckdorf in O'Neill's Hotel* (1969) and *Miss Gomez and the Brethren* (1971) he went on collecting ageing characters in a hotel or hostel situation with one catalytic outsider, a female photographer who turns out to be mad or a Jamaican ex-prostitute hooked on religion. In *Elizabeth Alone* (1973) he uses a hospital to group four women together—a forty-one-year-old divorcee condemned to hysterectomy, an old woman and two young women.

With more media available to our writers than ever before, surprisingly few of them are making it their business to explore more than one or two of them. William Trevor was a sculptor until, at the age of thirty-five, he turned to writing, and, arguably, he is still a sculptor in the way he re-shapes his plastic fictions to fit different media. He has developed short

William Trevor

stories into novels and plays for radio, theatre and television. *The Old Boys*, which was staged in 1971, had been a story (1963) before it became a novel. His television play *The Mark-2 Wife* was also first written as a story and it appears in his 1972 collection *The Ballroom of Romance*. Like *Elizabeth Alone*, his collection of stories *Angels at the Ritz* (1975) shows that his excursions into other media have helped to increase both precision and freedom of movement in his fiction, while there is a closer interpenetration between macabre fantasy and meticulous observation.

Malcolm Bradbury is another novelist who has profited from writing for television. His play *The After Dinner Game* (1975, written in collaboration with Christopher Bigsby) introduced some of the characters who appear in his novel *The History Man*, which came out later in the year. After a novel set in a redbrick university (*Eating People Is Wrong*, 1959) and one about an English novelist's adventures on an American campus (*Stepping Westward*, 1965), *The History Man* is set in a new English university, housed in depersonalizing concrete buildings designed by a Finnish architect. It has plexiglass domes, uniform corridors and plastic tables. But none of the three books is merely a novel about a university, and *The History Man* brilliantly encapsulates ten years of British social and cultural history. When the university opened, some of the teaching was done in Watermouth Hall. The old country house has since been replaced by an office block, while Kaakinen's concrete campus encroaches further and further on the English countryside and radical sociologists convince themselves that they are on the side of history as they apply totalitarian methods to furthering the cause of social revolution inside the university.

Malcolm Bradbury has written: 'What Jane Austen must do in *Emma* and *Persuasion*, as in any serious novel of social and moral realism, is to create and complexly to connect a society and a moral life.' His own novels are in the tradition of Jane Austen, E. M. Forster and Angus Wilson. The influence of Evelyn Waugh is more superficial, but the surface is as scintillatingly amusing as Waugh's, which makes it safe for Bradbury to be much more serious underneath. He is profoundly concerned at having to watch what Forster called 'the fag end of Victorian liberalism' being squashed under the steamroller of radical conformism. The Kirks, the central couple in *The History Man*, are 'true citizens of the present'. Howard wears a Zapata moustache and a sweatshirt with a rousing symbol on it; Barbara wears frizzled blonde hair and no bra. Both are as high-minded in their unscrupulousness as their fellow-guerrillas in the war against individualism. 'You mean there's no me any more?' asks an American woman. 'You're there, you're present,' answers Howard, 'but you happen to be a conjunction of known variables, cultural, psychological, genetic.'

The radical egalitarians who use history as an argument deny history as a fact, doing their utmost to abolish the past in their style of living and in their attitude to property. Appropriately, the novel is written in the present tense. This never becomes tedious, partly because the very good jokes are textured so densely. It is quite a long novel, but it fills only 230 pages because it runs dialogue on inside the paragraph instead of starting a new line for each speech.

Howard Kirk's most promising adversary is the attractive Miss Callendar, a Scots-accented lecturer in English Literature. 'I don't believe in group virtue,' she insists. 'It seems to me such an individual achievement.' The novel's main weakness is in letting her capitulate to Howard's sexual dominion without either putting up a better resistance or staging an ideological recovery. But there is an admirable mixture of accuracy and irony in spotlighting what goes on inside the Sociology Department of the university. At the departmental meeting, for instance, in the Durkheim Room of the Social Science Building, student representatives propose that representatives of the 'tea-ladies' should be co-opted.

After training at one of our best drama schools, Paul Bailey worked as an actor from 1956–63 before applying his powers of empathy to fiction.

His first novel, *At the Jerusalem* (1967) is about an old woman in a geriatric home. In his second, *Trespasses* (1970) the fragmented text reflects the central character's breakdown, which follows his wife's suicide. At first the arrangement of fragments seems random—memories, conversations, dreams, passages of free association. But it throws up a pattern of clues. We see why she came to feel so rejected; we also see how the reintegration of his personality begins.

9

BERYL BAINBRIDGE SUSAN HILL BERNICE RUBENS

As fought in Beryl Bainbridge's intriguing novels, the sex war usually involves killing. In *Harriet Said . . .*, which was written nearly fifteen years before it was published in 1972, two sisters spy on a neighbour as he makes love to his wife. Eventually one kills him but the other is to blame. In *The Dressmaker* (1973) the initial aggression comes from some American soldiers who enjoy baiting Liverpool women. When a GI makes love to a fifty-year-old, her jealous sister stabs him with a pair of scissors. After the corpse has been put into a bag made from a curtain, a man is briefed to drop it in the Mersey. In *The Bottle Factory Outing* (1974) the victim is female and the killing accidental, though still associated with sexual violence. Again there is a problem about how to dispose of the corpse. The Italian bottle factory workers push it into a barrel marked 'Tainted' and ship it to Santander, hoping it will be dumped overboard. Treated archly, these plots would be insufferable, but Beryl Bainbridge writes with subtlety and humane warmth.

Sweet William (1975) is the only one of her recent novels in which no one dies. A vulnerable girl becomes hopelessly involved with an unpredictable Scottish playwright just after her fiancé has left for America. She discovers that she is pregnant, and he seems sincere each time he renews his promise to leave his other woman and his other children to live with her and her baby. A series of disconcerting discoveries about him is ironically topped by the revelation that he is not the author of the pregnancy. The well-judged verbal economy strengthens each comic point.

Beryl Bainbridge has evolved a stylish blend of humour, pathos, charm, accuracy and directness in describing human indignities.

One of our most prolific novelists, Susan Hill is capable of exceptional intensity. She seems to be fascinated by relationships that involve either close friendship or extreme animosity between two males. *I'm the King of the Castle* (1970) centres on a territorial battle between two ten-year-old schoolboys; in *Strange Meeting* (1971) she almost overtaxes her powers of empathy in telling the story of an intimate friendship between two English subalterns in France during the 1914–18 war; *The Bird of Night* (1972) chronicles the male narrator's nurse-like devotion to a major poet who is mentally unbalanced. Formidable though it is, her technical prowess is not yet adequate to the formidable tasks she sets herself.

Bernice Rubens's novel *The Elected Member* (1969, which won the Booker Prize in 1970) looks at a Rabbi's household in the light of Ronald Laing's observation that if a patient is disturbed, it may be because the family is disturbing. Some of the behaviour and some of the dialogue of these characters is unconvincing. The Rabbi's locutions are contrived by amputating the word *it*. 'Is not far from here.' Bernice Rubens grinds her gears at some of the diversions into flashback, but there is also a pungent blend of comedy and pathos in the picture of the ingrown brother-sister relationship. The unmarried girl stays at home; her barrister brother takes to drugs and hallucinations. Eventually he accuses God of bloody-mindedness.

This was the fourth of Bernice Rubens's novels to use a Jewish background. Her fifth, *Sunday Best* (1971), is about a transvestite who regularly indulges in his vice on Sundays. *Go Tell the Lemming* (1973) is reminiscent of Muriel Spark's *The Public Image*. A husband is successful in the film world while his wife works in a Soho cutting-room. When the action shifts to Italy, it becomes apparent that to him private crises are only raw material for publicity. Compared with Muriel Spark's neat craftsmanship and subtle comedy, Bernice Rubens's use of violence seems uneconomical, and the climax is too much like a sick joke—marriage with a horror film monster. The main structural device in *I Sent a Letter to My Love* (1975) is also like a sick joke. To save herself from wasting her whole life on her crippled brother, a middle-aged spinster advertises in the Lonely Hearts column of a local newspaper. The only reply she gets is from him. Equally desperate for love, they have only each other. As in *The Elected Member*, the underlying obsession with incest is not fully explored.

10

Africa, White and Black

NADINE GORDIMER CHINUA ACHEBE AMOS TUTUOLA AYI KWEI ARMAH

Jonathan Raban has suggested that 'Perhaps the most remarkable thing about African fiction is the way that Africa itself spreads and moulds into the form of the packed, complicated, densely structured nineteenth-century novel.' Both in South Africa and in the Black states, social mobility is generally more limited than it is in the West, so observation of manners in the novel is more functional. At the same time the writer is pressured into assuming a more didactic role. Nadine Gordimer's achievement, therefore, is all the more remarkable in moving, effectively, from the nineteenth century to the twentieth within the six years it took her to write *A Guest of Honour* (1971) and *The Conservationist* (1974). After confining herself to the privacy of personal relationships in her novel *The Late Bourgeois World* (1966), she moved out into public affairs, building *A Guest of Honour* around the conflict between the President of a Black state and his Marxist adversary. The guest of honour is a liberal Colonel, whose short-sightedness, like many of Nadine Gordimer's details, takes on rich overtones of significance.

This also happens in *The Conservationist*, in which Mehring, a South African businessman in his late forties, wants to preserve as much as he can of the wild life on his expense-account farm, and of the privilege that his white skin earns him. His Sunday peace is disturbed by an abandoned black corpse that loses none of its physical actuality in its symbolical penumbra. It has appeared out of the flood waters. No one is concerned about it. Eventually it is buried by the police. Dickensian ramifications were generously allowed in *A Guest of Honour*; here they are pruned back: this is the most economical, most experimental and most poetic of Miss Gordimer's novels.

Quotations from *The Religious System of the Amazulu* by Revd Henry Callaway are embroidered into the text, richly juxtaposing fragments of native lore against narrative and dialogue which chronicle the moment-to-

Nadine Gordimer

moment existence of the unperceptive conservationist, who is really taking all he can from the life that surrounds him. The criticism put in the mouth of his radical girlfriend is sometimes unnecessarily explicit, but his sexual dominion over her parallels the domination he wants over the land, while Miss Gordimer makes subtle use of his son's embarrassment at his behaviour towards the blacks.

'My politics', says Chinua Achebe, 'are concerned with universal human communication across racial and cultural boundaries as a means of fostering respect for all people.' His fourth novel, *A Man of the People* (1966), is his most overtly political. Its accuracy in prophesying the Nigerian civil war, which broke out only a month after its publication, has distracted attention from his progressive refinement of his narrative techniques. Unlike his first novel *Things Fall Apart* (1958), his second, *No Longer at Ease* (1960), was satirical; the satire in *A Man of the People* is very much more sophisticated. Insincerity is exposed directly through language. With the corrupt politicians, like Chief the Hon. M. A. Nanga, this is easily accomplished, but the narrator too, Odili, is made to condemn himself unwittingly by the way he uses words. Language is one of Achebe's main subjects. Odili can recognize what is phoney in the politicians' cheap bids for popularity and in the second-hand phrases of the letter he receives from the girl who has rejected him in favour of the wily old chief, but his conceit at the power he has acquired over the English language is made into a clear index of his superficiality.

At the same time, Achebe was desperately anxious about administrative and political corruption in Nigeria. Embezzlement among the civil service was only part of the problem: in winning independence, the country seemed to have gained nothing real. As he put it himself, 'The old white master was still in power. He had got himself a bunch of black stooges to do his dirty work for a commission. As long as they did what was expected of them they would be praised for their sagacity and their country for its stability.'

For the creative writer working in the English language, the problem was how to filter his awareness of what was going on through words and phrases that had been minted to express the attitudes of the white master. The African has experiences, emotions, sensations, which never occur outside Africa and therefore have no counterparts in non-African languages.

When the civil war started, Chinua Achebe worked for Biafra, and the new novel he had started 'seemed unimportant compared with what was happening'. Of the thirteen stories in *Girls at War* (1972) only three were new, and five date from the fifties. The title story shows how the war debases an idealistic young militant into a venal good-time girl.

Amos Tutuola has been called[1] 'the most African of African writers'. He has been accused of borrowing techniques of fable-making from Dante, Blake and Bunyan, while he undeniably takes images from Western technology, but the main influences are Yoruba. As Bernth Lindfors has demonstrated,[2] his sources are not only oral: he has also borrowed extensively from the vernacular novels of Chief Daniel O. Fagunwa. The international reputation Tutuola achieved with *The Palm Wine Drinkard* (1952) embarrassed Nigerians whose syntax in English was more orthodox, but they are now more reconciled to his highly personal style of wrestling with the language. At least he is writing colourfully and entertainingly, as well as bridging effectively between oral tradition and literature.

The Beautyful Ones Are Not Yet Born by Ayi Kwei Armah, a Ghanaian who was still in his twenties when he finished it in 1968, must be one of the best novels to have come out of Africa. His extraordinary articulacy (sharpened at Harvard University and by experiences as a translator in Algeria and France) has been fired by his savage indignation about the

[1] Bernth Lindfors, 'Amos Tutuola's Television-Handed Ghostess' in *Readings in Commonwealth Literature*, edited by William Walsh, London, 1973.

[2] *Journal of Commonwealth Literature*, No. 9, 1970.

state of his country and wrought into a highly powerful prose. High praise from American critics did little to appease the resentment of Africans: many had the feeling that he was writing about Ghana as if he were a fastidious foreigner on a casual visit.

The overwhelming impression is one of disgust. Sensitive nostrils are twitching at a powerful stench. But Armah involves the reader in his nausea. The central imagery is of excrement. Drying urine trickles among pinched cigarette ends in wide gutters; the fart of a well-fed socialist politician fills the room as if it were a corrosive gas. 'The man', the anonymous central character, isolates himself by trying to resist the ubiquitous forces of corruption. He is compared by his materialistic wife, with the chichidodo, a bird that 'hates excrement with all its soul' but feeds only on maggots which 'grow best inside the lavatory'. The narrative provides some relief from the acrid atmosphere with sweeter-smelling memories of childhood, but in any case the story's momentum is strong enough to carry us through to the symbolic climax, which occurs after the fall of Nkrumah. The man is pressured into helping the fat politician in a desperate effort to escape head-first through the bowl of a dirty lavatory. But the novel ends with a return to routine. A bird is singing happily over the school latrine. 'But then suddenly all his mind was consumed with thoughts of everything he was going back to—Oyo, the eyes of the children after six o'clock, the office and every day, and above all the never-ending knowledge that this aching emptiness would be all that the remainder of his own life could offer him.'

Fiction like this can exist only by approaching over-explicitness, and in *Fragments* (1969) and *Why Are We So Blest?* (1972) the spokes sometimes poke through the fabric of the narrative umbrella. *Fragments* is flawed by strenuous efforts to be more positive and optimistic than he really wants to be. Both novels lack the urgent intensity and economy of *The Beautyful Ones Are Not Yet Born*, but the experiments in narrative technique are interesting, especially in *Why Are We So Blest?*, which is like Ruth Prawer Jhabvala's *A New Dominion* in providing a carefully structured sequence of short chapters narrated from several consciousnesses, male and female, coloured and white. The preoccupations of the character Solo are dangerously close to Armah's own, but Modin, the depressive African revolutionary, is very well drawn, and the viewpoint of his American girlfriend is effectively used in the vivid, nauseating account of the tortures inflicted on him.

11

Australia

PATRICK WHITE THOMAS KENEALLY

Patrick White's novels have deep roots in the nineteenth century and in modernism. He was born into an old Australian family (knowledge of which mediates his characters' memories of late Victorian society), and he read Modern Languages at Cambridge (where the French Symbolists made a lasting impression on him). One of the epigraphs to *The Vivisector* (1970) is Rimbaud's description of the artist: 'He becomes beyond all other the great Invalid, the great Criminal, the great Accursed One—and the Supreme Knower. For he reaches the unknown.'

White's novel *The Solid Mandala* (1966) is set in the Sydney suburb of Sarsaparilla and portrays twin brothers, Waldo and Arthur Brown, as contrasted examples of failure to come fully alive. Waldo aims at the detachment of the artist; Arthur responds to experience with a spontaneity that belongs to the early stage at which his development has been arrested. Innocent of the disgust that makes Waldo recoil from the physical facts of existence, Arthur stumbles inadvertently closer to fulfilling the artistic ambition represented by the Mandala, a symbol of totality: 'It is believed to be the "dwelling of the god". Its protective circle is a pattern of order superimposed on psychic chaos.'

The Vivisector brings the two halves together into a single artist, a painter, but a dichotomy is imposed by contrasting his early, penurious childhood with the opulence that ensues when the Courtneys, a rich couple with a hunchbacked daughter, pay five hundred pounds to adopt him. An impassioned anti-vivisectionist, Mrs Courtney renders him incapable of loving: all he will be able to do with his experience is vivisect it, making it into art. Patrick White's view of the artist's isolation sometimes seems more Rimbaudian or Baudelairean than Australian, and there are passages where the identification with Hurtle Duffield's viewpoint seems strained. The most interesting tensions are generated when he is in conversation with someone very unlike himself or when his values are thrown into dramatic conflict with those of average Australian vulgarians.

In *The Eye of the Storm* (1973) Patrick White turns away from the artist

Patrick White

and his problems to a rich old woman not unlike Mrs Courtney. Once a great beauty, she is dying in a suburban Sydney house. Hunter is her over-indicative surname and, as we learn from the skilfully organized flashbacks, she has lived as a predator, using her body and her charm to snap up people and possessions, but her compulsion to devour has been unaccompanied by any talent for enjoying. The victims include her two children, now middle-aged. Even at her death-bed they cannot defend themselves against the vitriolic malice that still flicks out from her tongue. Patrick White makes her totally convincing: it is even plausible that at the age of seventy she could still take a man away from her daughter.

Thomas Keneally published his first novel *A Place at Whitton* in 1964, when he was twenty-nine, and since then hardly a year has passed without the appearance of a new one. He describes his third, *Bring Larks and Heroes* (1967), as 'an attempt to follow out an epic theme in terms of a young soldier's exile to Australia'. *Three Cheers for the Paraclete* (1968) and *The Survivor* (1969) 'were attempts at urbane writing in the traditional mode of the English novel—confrontations with characters whose behaviour shows layers of irony and humour'. Of *A Dutiful Daughter* (1971) he said: 'I have turned to myth and fable, as many a novelist is doing, for the simple reason that other media have moved into the traditional areas of the novel.'

His style is as Protean as his output is profuse, but though he is lacking in neither energy nor inventiveness, some of his effects seem facile. Most of his novels are historical but he lacks J. G. Farrell's talent for seeding out tendencies from the present into a carefully cultivated patch of past. Neither the deliberate anachronisms in *Bring Larks and Heroes* nor the garish pictures of collective viciousness destroy the analogy between the eighteenth-century Australian penal colony and modern society, but few of the more recent novels have achieved comparable resonance. *Three Cheers for the Paraclete* draws on Thomas Keneally's experience of a seminary to show a progressive young priest in conflict with a hidebound Catholic community. *The Survivor* is less successful, using flashbacks to explore forty-year-old guilt feelings in the survivor of an Antarctic expedition. Before it set out he had an affair with the wife of the leader, who did not survive. In *A Dutiful Daughter* the girl's duties to her dairy-farming parents include veterinary attention after her first menstruation seems to have been partially responsible for transforming them into semi-bovine animals and her mother develops an infection of the udder.

After this, it was not surprising when Keneally turned from fable to history. *The Chant of Jimmy Blacksmith*, his novel published in 1972, which was short-listed for the Booker Prize, tells the story of an aborigine in New South Wales at the turn of the century. The theme is the 'rape of primitives' by the whites. *Blood Red, Sister Rose* (1974) anachronistically presents Joan of Arc as a peasant with a problem: 'He still thinks you're a cowboy, Jehanne. Show him your tits.' Some of the dialogue is written out as in a playscript, a device he repeats in *Gossip from the Forest*, which was also short-listed for the Booker Prize. It dramatizes the confrontation between the plenipotentiaries who met in railway coaches at Compiègne to sign the ceasefire in November 1918. As in Ruth Prawer Jhabvala's *A New Dominion*, narrative is broken up into short sections with titles, while the cutting is cinematic. Thanks to Keneally's powers of empathy, he is sometimes able to penetrate deeply and convincingly into the core of the experience, but the method tends to minimize the cumulative effect, while the anti-traditionalism is more apparent than real. He is even assuming the right to look inside the consciousness of all his characters.

12

New Zealand

FRANK SARGESON DAN DAVIN

'As a schoolboy,' says Frank Sargeson, 'I became much aware that I was a European, but in a country very remote from Europe.' E. M. Forster praised him for his commitment to 'the unsmart, the unregulated and the affectionate'. After including some of his stories of the 1940s in *New Writing*, John Lehmann published his second novel, *I Saw in My Dream* (1949). *The Hangover* (1967) was his fifth novel, an unrealistic story about a boy who finds himself out of sympathy both with the materialism of the Establishment and with the beatnik opposition to it. *Joy of the Worm* (1969) is about a self-important old Methodist minister who competes successfully against his son for a desirable widow. The Hemingwayish directness of the early stories has been eclipsed by an experimental-looking quirkiness of narrative manner, which belies the straightforwardness of the matter.

Dan Davin's sixth novel *Not Here, Not Now* (1970), the last in a sequence he had conceived in 1939, was the one he originally intended to write first, and it might have been better if he had. Set in New Zealand during the thirties, it now seems neither historical nor topical. *Brides of Price* (1972) is more richly textured. A leading anthropologist produces an intimate autobiography instead of the life-work greedily awaited by the academic world. Is guilt his personal aphrodisiac, he wonders? But the insight has no effect as an antidote, and there are virile accounts of his couplings.

13

Canada, Jewish and Catholic exiles

MORDECAI RICHLER BRIAN MOORE

'All my attitudes are Canadian,' said Mordecai Richler in 1957. He had left when he was twenty to live in Europe (mainly England) but he went on revisiting Canada, and his novels have been born legitimately enough out of the marriage between his sense of exile and his consciousness of being Jewish. The Jewish ghetto around St Urbain Street in Montreal is to him what Dublin was to Joyce. It is no longer the same as when he knew it, but he goes on writing about it.

At the opposite pole of the Richler world is the glamorous, moneyed, traditionless business of film-making. *Cocksure* (1968) is a persecution story with a film man as victim and a Jew, vengefully conscious of the historical pattern, as aggressor:

> 'I've resigned my job at Oriole.'
> 'Griffin, the scapegoat.'
> 'There are killers seeking me out even now.'
> 'Well, now you see, now you know. It's hard to be a Jew.'
> 'I am not,' Mortimer said, seizing Shalinsky by the shoulders and shaking him, 'a Jew.'
> 'But Griffin, Griffin, don't you see? A Jew is an idea. Today you're my idea of a Jew.'

St Urbain's Horseman (1971) cooks the same ingredients into a more ambitious dish. There is a strong flavour of autobiography in the nostalgic memories of a St Urbain Street childhood and in the guilt feelings that sabotage married life in England with a non-Jewess. There is also a spicy fantasy about a cousin, an idealized Jewish avenger against the persecuting world. The robust comic energy bubbles through to the racy surface of the narrative, and some of the satire is effective, even if the structure is not strong enough for such heterogeneous material. A degree of anarchy is acceptable if the story is kept in focus, but it isn't.

'The singular strength of Brian Moore's novels,' wrote Christopher Ricks, reviewing *The Emperor of Ice-Cream* (1966) in the *New Statesman*, 'is manifest in their abolishing brow-distinction . . . by concentrating simply, directly and bravely on the primary sufferings and passions that everybody feels.' This is equally true of the novels he has written since 1966—*I Am Mary Dunne* (1968), *Fergus* (1971), *The Revolution Script* and *Catholics* (both 1972) and *The Great Victorian Collection* (1975). But he would not have been able to concentrate in the way he has on the primary emotions if he had remained in Belfast, where he was born in 1921. He emigrated to Canada in 1948, giving up his British citizenship for Canadian, and in 1959 he moved to the United States, living in New York and California. He was born into a Catholic family and though he is no longer a Catholic himself, his tenth novel is the first to have a non-Catholic, non-Irish hero.

Since his first novel, *The Lonely Passion of Judith Hearne* (1955), isolation, exile, alienation, sexual frustration have been central themes. Again like Joyce, who took Dublin to Paris with him, Brian Moore has transported Irish Catholicism into North America, and Philip French[1] is right to call *The Great Victorian Collection* 'a survey of his own literary career and a shrewd allegory of the situation of the artist in contemporary society'. A Canadian don has written his PhD thesis on 'A Study of the Effects of Gaining a Colonial Empire on the Mores of Victorian England as Exemplified by the Art and Architecture of the Period'. After dreaming about a huge collection of invaluable Victoriana, he finds the objects have materialized in a vacant parking-lot next to the motel he was sleeping in. He has dreamed the objects up, but are they his? Is the writer a master or a copy-typist, plugged in permanently to the dictaphone provided by his own repetition compulsion, fictitiously conquering situations which have in reality defeated him and countries from which he has escaped? *The Great Victorian Collection* is an image that represents his cultural heritage, his talent, and his output. He is at first subject to anxiety that he may be unable to prevent it from disappearing; later to guilt feelings about allowing it to be exploited commercially.

One of the values of this extraordinary book is that it provides a skeleton key to doors in Brian Moore's earlier novels that may have remained closed. The middlebrow reader can make himself perfectly at home in *I Am Mary Dunne* without exploring the intellectual attic. There are several levels, all easily accessible, in the story of an attractive woman on the brink of suicide. The lifeline of continuity that connected her with her childhood has been damaged by three marriages, four surnames, bouts of amnesia, disturbing confrontations with strangers and friends—desperate, predatory, lecherous, accusing. It was the first novel Brian Moore had written entirely in the first person, and he succeeded spectacularly in empathizing with a woman who had lost her sense of identity after presenting three different personalities to each of her husbands. But no man could have understood her so well without suffering identity anxieties of his own.

Fergus is a success as a novelist and a failure as a husband. Living in California with a young girl, he is visited by ghosts—parents, recriminating

[1] *The Times Literary Supplement*, 17 October 1975.

priest, spinsterish aunt, boyhood self, women he'd desired and Ulster policemen—who involve him in unpleasant conversations about the past he had tried to slough off into fiction. Fergus, like Brian Moore, lives in a house on the Californian beach. The book interweaves the fictions of the real and fictitious selves. Fergus has been at the same school as the central character in Moore's *The Feast of Lupercal* (1956), and there is a girl called Una, as there was in *The Lonely Passion of Judith Hearne*.

The Revolution Script appears to be a documentary novel about the kidnapping of James Cross by the Quebec Liberation Front in 1970. It seldom looks inside the consciousness of the characters and it is straightforward, but it is also haunted by the ghost of his Belfast boyhood.

Catholics, like *The Great Victorian Collection*, is a wry fable which exposes some of the absurdities in current cultural trends. It is set in the immediate future on the Isle of Muck, where rebelliously traditionalist Irish monks are defying the Vatican and continuing to celebrate the Mass as a miracle. A helicopter brings an emissary from the Holy See—an American, Father Kinsella, who has been profoundly influenced by the doctrines of the Guevara-like South-American priest, Gustav Hartman. Christianity can have a future if it gets rid of God. There is an effective twist in the story when the Abbot, leader of the insular resistance, turns out to have lost his faith. But he still puts a high value on the comfort offered by the old rituals.

In this brief account of them I may have placed too much emphasis on the thematic continuity between the novels. Brian Moore has been admirable in his determination never to repeat himself and each book is refreshingly different from its predecessors.

14
India

MULK RAJ ANAND R. K. NARAYAN KAMALA MARKANDAYA

Born in the first decade of the twentieth century, Anand and Narayan both belong essentially to the nineteenth, and neither has been very productive recently. According to Saros Cowasjee, both Anand's *Morning Face* (1968) and his *The Private Life of an Indian Prince* (1953), which he revised in 1970, are autobiographical. The Prince's breakdown is very much like one that Anand suffered himself when he returned to India after twenty years in England and had an affair in Bombay with a woman who left him. The story of the Prince fuses personal and political themes, showing the effects of Independence on an Indian state.

Narayan has been praised for creating a novelistic community comparable in solidity to William Faulkner's Yoknapatawpha. *Mr Sampath* (1949), the first in Narayan's sequence of novels centred on Malgudi, was written when he was forty-three. At the end of his most recent full-length novel, *The Sweet Vendor* (1967), the central character, Jagan, withdraws from life in the community—from 'a set of repetitions performed for sixty years'—to assist a stonemason in carving a statue of a goddess. 'I am going to watch a goddess come out of a stone.' As Shirley Chew has pointed out,[1] this withdrawal represents a movement into the third of the four stages in life's pilgrimage as defined by the Hindu theory of *asrama*. The main objective of this stage is to escape from the bustle of life into solitary meditation on the higher problems. But in objectifying the routines of community life and of Jagan's working life as a sweet vendor, the novel provides ample evidence of the bustle, while Narayan's prose preserves its fastidious calm.

Kamala Markandaya published her first novel *Nectar in a Sieve* in 1954. As William Walsh has put it,[2] 'She is preoccupied with the opposition between a cerebral, Western—and she seems to be suggesting, a narrowly Benthamite—habit of mind and the more inclusive, the more ancient and ritualistic Indian sensibility.' Her novel *The Coffer Dams* (1969) describes British engineers working in India on building a dam. Indian critics took her to task for lack of empathy with the poor. Her novel *Two Virgins* (1974) is more private. After years of quiet life in an Indian village, a beautiful girl is tempted away by a film director's promises of stardom. The story is told from the viewpoint of her younger sister, who is plainer and more placid. The delicately textured prose seems to grow richer as the story proceeds.

[1] 'A Proper Detachment: The Novels of R. K. Narayan', *Southern Review*, June 1972.

[2] *Commonwealth Literature*, London, 1973

15

The West Indies and British Guiana

V. S. NAIPAUL SHIVA NAIPAUL WILSON HARRIS GEORGE LAMMING ANDREW SALKEY SAMUEL SELVON

'What's nationality these days?' asks the English tramp on a Greek steamer in the Prologue to V. S. Naipaul's *In a Free State*. 'I myself, I think of myself as a citizen of the world.' Naipaul was born in Trinidad of Indian parents, and since his Oxford education he has mostly lived in England, determined to write, but always experiencing extreme difficulty in finding a centre to write from. 'All the novels I had read were about settled and organized societies, and I was aware of a slight fraudulence in applying a form created by that type of society to the squalor, disorder and shallowness of my own.' His novelistic techniques are elaborate barricades which distract attention from the empty centre of the garrison they are defending; his perspectives are based on shifting horizons.

The success of *The Mimic Men* (1967) showed that readers of very different backgrounds could identify with the forty-year-old ex-politician Ralph Singh, who can feel at home neither in London nor on the Caribbean island where he was born. If Naipaul was innovating, it was not so much in form as in the tone of this painful alienation comedy. After three abortive, twenty thousand-word efforts at writing the story chronologically, he found it could be made to work only if he began in the middle, with Singh writing his memoirs in a London suburb. The narrative achieves its balance by finding a rhythm and a wry resignation in its own restlessness as it shuttles backwards and forwards through an elaborate series of failures, personal and political. For Singh, as for the book, wholeness is achieved through the process of putting memories into order.

Naipaul is unique among Caribbean writers. He has drawn elegantly on the inelegancies of West Indian English, preserving a fastidious but effortless-seeming poise between comedy that verges on farce and his near-tragic vision of the human frustrations endemic in a world of exiles and guerrillas. A watershed seems to occur in his fiction between *The Mimic Men* and *In a Free State* (1971). Light-heartedness has not disappeared altogether from his seventies work, but it is less prominent. The ironies

V. S. Naipaul

are fiercer, the observation tuned more harshly to the oppressive elements in the environment and the distasteful elements in human physicality. His development as a novelist may have been influenced by his non-fiction; his honesty in reporting his own impressions tends to limit the independence of his characters: they respond to everything with his sensitivity.

The ironically ambiguous title *In a Free State* applies to Naipaul as much as to the characters in the stories. By beginning and ending the volume with excerpts from a diary he is emphasizing his affinity with them: none of them belongs to the cultural and political background we see them in, but they are free mainly in the sense of drifting, while the states concede even less freedom to their citizens.

In 'One Out of Many', the first story, the narrator is Santosh, a cook who has been brought to Washington from Bombay. His Anglo-Indian style reads almost like a parody of Narayan, but again the tone is exactly right for the rueful, uncomfortable comedy of displacement. The *novella*-length title story is set in Africa. Angus Calder wrote in his *New Statesman* review:[1] 'I don't know any writer since Conrad who's exposed the otherness of Africa so starkly . . . While the adjacent territory of Greeneland is one where heroism may just be possible and revolt might just be successful, Naipaulia remains a kingdom of cryptic anti-climax.' In a new Black state, one tribe is killing off another, while the whites—a bitchy Englishwoman and a homosexual civil servant on the look-out for black lovers—do not deserve the safety their colour guarantees them. The action is sharp, dramatic; the writing abrasive.

In 1972 Michael Malik (alias Michael de Freitas alias Michael X), who had been a Black Power leader in England, was condemned to death in Trinidad for murdering a man. He had also been charged with murdering an Englishwoman, Gale Benson, a divorcee who had been living in a Trinidad commune with another Black Power leader, a Boston Negro who had taken the Muslim name of Hakim Jamal. V. S. Naipaul went back to the island and wrote a long, two-part article on the case for *The Sunday Times Magazine*. He then used the three central characters as the basis for his novel *Guerrillas* (1975) which powerfully projects a sense of personal centrelessness into all three principals. Partly Chinese, James Ahmed has always been guiltily confused between feeling superior and feeling inferior to the Blacks among whom he grew up. For the Black Power leader Naipaul substitutes a white South African, Peter Roche, who has perpetrated acts of sabotage against the Vorster government. He is living uneasily on an un-named West Indian island with an Englishwoman, Jane. John Spurling has suggested in *Encounter* (December 1975) that the names may allude to Rochester and Jane Eyre and that Ahmed may be compared with Heathcliff. She feels ashamed of her own privileged life and rightly senses an inadequacy at the core of her lover: his courageous acts of sabotage have been motivated by his own sense of shame. Nevertheless, despite his debt to the facts of the Malik case, Naipaul has extended his range and increased the depth of his characterization by distributing his own sense of homelessness between three such contrasted characters, all unlike him.

[1] 8 October 1971.

His brother, Shiva Naipaul (who is fourteen years younger) has written two extremely accomplished novels: *Fireflies* (1970) and *The Chip-Chip Gatherers* (1973). A large Indian family with some resemblances to his own is used in *Fireflies* with a likeable mixture of affection and irony as a microcosm of Trinidad life. *The Chip-Chip Gatherers* is more selective in its detail and more inclined to focus on the poor, who laboriously gather chip-chip shells for food. They are 'the size and shape of a long fingernail'. If critics have recourse to the word 'Dickensian' in describing Shiva Naipaul's work, the reason lies partly in his need to be explicit about dynastic family relationships and about local customs and institutions; there is also a Dickensian richness in his descriptions of family rituals. Even eating meals has an element of ritual in it.

Wilson Harris, formerly a government surveyor, has an intimate knowledge of the British Guianian landscape, which bulks large in the consciousness of his characters, though in some of his later work much of the action is internal. 'The creative human consolation', he has said,[1] 'lies in the search for a kind of inward dialogue and space when one is deprived of a ready conversational tongue and hackneyed comfortable approach.'

Tumatumari (1968) dramatizes the opposition between primeval and progressive elements inside the imagination. *Ascent to Omai* (1970) develops the traditional analogy between the world and the human brain. *Black Marsden* (1972) is an extravaganza which uses magic and mysticism in a much more light-hearted way than his early novels, breaking away from the obscurity that had bedevilled them. The character who narrates is called Clive Goodrich and the story is about his adventures in Edinburgh with a 'ritual conjuror' called Black Marsden. *Companions of the Day and Night* (1975) is dedicated to Margaret and the memory of B. S. Johnson. The 'Editor's Introduction', which is signed by Clive Goodrich, imputes the authorship of the 'voluminous papers and diaries' on which the novel is based to Black Marsden. The narrative is divided into short sections, titled according to a motif taken from the pre-Columbian calendar, and it ends with a letter from Black Marsden.

George Lamming made a great impact with his first novel, *In the Castle of My Skin* (1953), and had written three more novels and a book of essays by the end of the decade, but an eleven-year gap supervened before the

[1] In a lecture on 'Tradition and the West Indian Novel' delivered to the London West Indian Students' Union in 1964 and published in *Tradition, the Writer and Society*. London, 1967.

publication of *Water with Berries* (1971), a story of three West Indian exiles in London—a painter, a composer and an actor. It is overheated with self-indulgent fantasies, over-written and overloaded with Shakespearean parallels.

Andrew Salkey's *The Late Emancipation of Jerry Stover* (1968) is set in Jamaica and it shows young people dissipating their energy, unable to benefit from their newly won independence. *The Adventures of Catullus Kelly* (1969) is set in London, and it squanders too much space on building up the hero as a man who finds that grateful prostitutes give him back his money. Random experiences with swinging young librarians and rambling conversations about the colour problem are sewn too loosely together. *Come Home, Malcolm Heartland* (1972) is better, but not so good as his first novel, *A Quality of Violence* (1959), which dealt with primitive peasants in Jamaica at the beginning of the century. *Anancy's Score* (1973) is about a spider—a series of Aesopian stories overweighted with political messages.

Samuel Selvon is, like the Naipauls, a Trinidadian of Indian extraction. He has lived in London for twenty-five years. After starting out as a short story writer, he soon found a way of applying semi-literate Caribbean English to comic, novel-length explorations of the West Indian immigrants' problems. His novel *Those Who Eat the Cascadura* (1972) was full of clichés, both in plot and in style, but his 1975 novel *Moses Ascending* revives the hero of *The Lonely Londoners* (1956), promoting him to the status of a landlord with a white menial. His mentality has also taken on a whitish hue: he calls the RSPCA when Pakistanis slaughter a sheep in the back yard. But the language remains joyfully unorthodox: 'And I record with pride that I wasn't one of them prejudiced landlord what put No Kolors on their notices. Come one, come all, first come, first served, was my mottos.'

16
Not a conclusion

Critics and historians of the novel generally pay too little attention to the consumer and to conditions prevailing in the market. So do authors. A poll taken in 1972 indicated that 56 per cent were earning less than £500 a year from their books. Like actors, they have a high threshold of resistance to the financial penalties imposed on them by an unreasoningly ambivalent society, which mingles envious admiration with Puritanic disapproval: why should anyone be paid for something he enjoys doing?

Unlike actors, who always have the option of working in pubs and cellars, novelists have no chance of putting their work in front of the public without a substantial investment of capital. To produce 1600 copies of a 160-page book in 1975 cost £1420—about three times as much as it did four years earlier. If all 1600 copies were sold, about 1400 would have been bought by libraries. Assuming that the price was £3.50 and that the average library copy will have been read forty times before it falls to pieces, the author's total earnings from his ten per cent royalty remain at £560, though the book will have been read by 56,200 people including the 200 who have paid for their copy.

As Lord Willis said in a speech to the House of Lords (4 July 1975) on the Public Lending Right, 'Borrowing and reading books is our most popular national pastime.' In the United States fourteen books are bought for every thirteen borrowed; in Britain there is a ratio of four purchases to thirty-eight loans. The public libraries make an average of 600,000,000 free loans every year, with novels accounting for 73 per cent of this tremendous turnover.

This absurd system is brutally damaging not only to the writer's standard of living but to his standard of writing. As John Sutherland has pointed out,[1] the borrower wants 'the kind of novel of which four or five can be read in a fortnight (one might also suggest, tentatively, that it is the two-week, six-book lending rule which has produced the noticeable shortness of the English novel compared to its American counterpart).' The novelist may be unconscious of how far he is being conditioned to cater for the requirements of his non-paying public, but he can scarcely be immune to the deterrents against writing slowly or at great length, and against making heavy demands on the reader's powers of imagination and concentration.

It is remarkable that in spite of these pressures on him to become less of an artist and more of an entertainer, so much good work is being produced. We are constantly being told that the novel is dead or dying, but even if there are no great novelists writing today, there is a great variety of

[1] 'Hard Times for the Novel', *The New Review*, Vol. 2. No. 18, September 1975.

extremely interesting ones who have so far succeeded in maintaining high standards. In the next few years it is likely to be even more difficult for them. Prices are continuing to rise and budgets to be cut back. Libraries are allocating a smaller proportion of their funds to fiction, while the number of private buyers is becoming almost negligible. There is no doubt that the novel will survive. The questions are: 'In what form?' and 'How far will its standards be forced down?'

It would help if more people became more conscious of the value they are effectively setting on the novel's social function. The idea that film and television are 'better' media for realistic story-telling ought finally to be discredited. It makes no more sense than the old assumption that photography would make painting redundant. A film sequence of a man strangling his wife is no more 'real' than a verbal description: it merely requires less effort from the audience because it is easier to watch moving pictures than to use words on a page as a stimulus to forming mental pictures of one's own. The one encouraging fact about library statistics is the reassurance they provide that so many people still enjoy forming their own pictures.

The novel, says Philippe Sollers, is the way in which society talks to itself. 'Our identity depends on the novel, what others think of us, what we think of ourselves, the way in which our life is imperceptibly moulded into a whole. How do others see us if not as a character from a novel?'[1] It would be much too facile to answer 'As a character from a film or a television play,' because the element of discourse is lacking from these media. What we want from fiction is not just a story but a story with a meaning. Dialogue is not always enough.

[1] *Logiques*, Paris, 1968.

Select Reading List

The list includes novelists who have published work in the period 1967–75. Each heading gives the following details: author, date of birth and nationality (where known), titles of novels, publisher and date of first hardback edition, publishers and dates of paperback editions, and place of publication if other than London.

ABSE, Dannie (1923–) British
Ash on a Young Man's Sleeve (Hutchinson, 1954; Corgi, 1972). *Some Corner of an English Field* (Hutchinson, 1956). *O. Jones, O. Jones* (Hutchinson, 1970; Corgi, 1974).

ACHEBE, Chinua (1930–) Nigerian
Things Fall Apart (Heinemann, 1958; Heinemann Educ., 1962). *No Longer at Ease* (Heinemann, 1960; Heinemann Educ., 1963). *The Sacrificial Egg, and Other Stories* (Etudo, Onitsha, 1962). *Arrow of God* (Heinemann, 1964; Heinemann Educ., 1966). *A Man of the People* (Heinemann, 1966; Heinemann Educ., 1966). *Girls at War, and Other Stories* (Heinemann, 1972; Heinemann Educ., 1972).

ADAMS, Richard
Watership Down (Collings, 1972; Penguin, 1973). *Shardik* (Allen Lane, Collings, 1974).

ALVAREZ, A. (1929–) British
Hers (Weidenfeld & Nicolson, 1974).

AMIS, Kingsley (1922–) British
Lucky Jim (Gollancz, 1954; Penguin, 1961; Longmans, 1963; Macmillan [abridged], 1967). *That Uncertain Feeling* (Gollancz, 1955; Panther, 1975). *I Like It Here* (Gollancz, 1958; Four Square, 1961; Penguin, 1968; Panther, 1975). *Take a Girl like You* (Gollancz, 1960; Penguin, 1970). *My Enemy's Enemy* (Gollancz, 1962). *One Fat Englishman* (Gollancz, 1963; Penguin, 1975). *The Egyptologists* [with Robert Conquest] (Cape, 1965; Penguin, 1968; Panther, 1975). *The Anti-Death League* (Gollancz, 1966; Penguin, 1968). *Colonel Sun: A James Bond Adventure* [as Robert Markham] (Cape, 1968; Pan, 1970). *I Want It Now* (Cape, 1968; Panther, 1970). *The Green Man* (Cape, 1969; Panther, 1972). *Girl, 20* (Cape, 1971; Panther, 1973). *Dear Illusion* (Covent Garden Press, 1972). *The Riverside Villas Murder* (Cape, 1973; Panther, 1974). *Ending Up* (Cape, 1974).

AMIS, Martin
The Rachel Papers (Cape, 1973). *Dead Babies* (Cape, 1975).

ANAND, Mulk Raj (1905–) Indian
The Lost Child, and Other Stories (J. A. Allen, 1934). *Untouchable* (Wishart, 1935). *Coolie* (Lawrence & Wishart, 1936; Bodley Head, 1972). *Two Leaves and a Bud* (Lawrence & Wishart, 1937). *The Village* (Cape, 1939). *Lament on the Death of a Master of Arts* (Kitabistan: Allahabad, 1939). *Across the Black Waters* (Cape, 1940). *The Sword and the Sickle* (Cape, 1942). *The Barber's Trade Union, and Other Stories* (Cape, 1944). *The Big Heart* (Hutchinson, 1945). *The Tractor and the Corn Goddess, and Other Stories* (Thacker: Bombay, 1947). *Seven Summers: The Story of an Indian Childhood* (Hutchinson, 1951). *The Private Life of an Indian Prince* (Hutchinson, 1953; revised ed. 1970). *Reflections on the Golden Bed* (Current Book House: Bombay, 1954). *The Road* (Kutub: Bombay, 1962). *The Old Woman and the Cow* (Kutub: Bombay, 1963). *Death of a Hero* (Kutub: Bombay, 1964). *The Power of Darkness* (Jaico: Bombay, 1966). *Morning Face* (Kutub: Bombay, 1968).

ANTHONY, Michael (1932–) Trinidadian
The Games were Coming (Deutsch, 1963). *The Year in San Fernando* (Deutsch, 1965; Heinemann, 1970). *Green Days by the River* (Deutsch, 1967; Heinemann, 1973). *Cricket in the Road* [short stories] (Deutsch, 1973).

ARMAH, Ayi Kwei (1939–) Ghanaian
The Beautyful Ones Are Not Yet Born (Heinemann, 1969; Heinemann Educ., 1969). *Fragments* (Houghton Mifflin, Boston, 1970; Heinemann Educ., 1974). *Why are We So Blessed* (Doubleday, 1972; Heinemann Educ., 1974).

BAILEY, Paul (1937–) British
At the Jerusalem (Cape, 1967; Panther, 1969). *Trespasses* (Cape, 1970). *A Distant Likeness* (Cape, 1973).

BAINBRIDGE, Beryl (1933–) British
A Weekend with Claud (New Authors, 1967; Panther, 1971). *Another Part of the Wood* (Hutchinson, 1968). *Harriet Said . . .* (Duckworth, 1972; Quartet Books, 1973). *The Dressmaker* (Duckworth, 1973; Fontana, 1974). *The Bottle Factory Outing* (Duckworth, 1974). *Sweet William* (Duckworth, 1975).

BARKER, Audrey Lilian (1918–) British
Innocents: Variations on a Theme (Hogarth Press, 1947). *Apology for a Hero* (Hogarth Press, 1950). *Novelette, with Other Stories* (Hogarth Press, 1951). *The Joy-Ride and After* (Hogarth Press, 1963). *Lost upon the Roundabouts* (Hogarth Press, 1964). *A Case Examined* (Hogarth Press, 1965). *The Middling: Chapters in the Life of Ellie Toms* (Hogarth Press, 1967; Penguin, 1969). *John Brown's Body* (Hogarth Press, 1969). *Femina Real* (Hogarth Press, 1971). *A Source of Embarrassment* (Hogarth Press, 1974).

BARSTOW, Stan (1928–) British
A Kind of Loving (Michael Joseph, 1960; Hutchinson, 1966; Corgi, 1973). *The Desperadoes and Other Stories* (Michael Joseph, 1961; Corgi, 1973). *Ask Me Tomorrow* (Michael Joseph, 1962; Corgi, 1974). *Joby* (Michael Joseph, 1964;

Penguin; 1968, Corgi, 1973). *The Watchers on the Shore* (Michael Joseph, 1966; Penguin, 1968; Corgi, 1974). *A Raging Calm* (Michael Joseph, 1968; Corgi, 1970). *The Human Element, and Other Stories* (Longman, 1970). *A Season with Eros* (Michael Joseph, 1971; Corgi, 1973).

BELBEN, Rosalind

Bogies: Two Stories (New Authors, 1972). *Reuben Little Hero* (Hutchinson pbk, 1973). *The Limit* (Hutchinson, 1974).

BERGER, John (1926–) British

A Painter of Our Time (Secker & Warburg, 1958). *The Foot of Clive* (Methuen, 1962; Penguin, 1971). *Corker's Freedom* (Methuen, 1964). *G* (Weidenfeld & Nicolson, 1972; Penguin, 1973).

BOWEN, Elizabeth (1899–1973) Irish

Encounters: Stories (Sidgwick and Jackson, 1923). *Ann Lee's and Other Stories* (Sidgwick and Jackson, 1926). *The Hotel* (Constable, 1927). *The Last September* (Constable, 1929). *Joining Charles and Other Stories* (Constable, 1929). *Friends and Relations* (Constable, 1931). *To the North* (Gollancz, 1932). *The Cat Jumps and Other Stories* (Gollancz, 1934). *The House in Paris* (Gollancz, 1935). *The Death of the Heart* (Gollancz, 1938; Penguin, 1962). *Look at All Those Roses: Short Stories* (Gollancz, 1941). *The Demon Lover and Other Stories* (Cape, 1945). *Selected Stories* (Fridberg, Dublin, 1946). *The Heart of the Day* (Cape, 1949; Penguin, 1962). *A World of Love* (Cape, 1955). *Stories* (Knopf, New York, 1959) *The Little Girls* (Cape, 1964). *A Day in the Dark and Other Stories* (Cape, 1965). *Eva Trout; or, Changing Scenes* (Cape, 1969).

BRADBURY, Malcolm (1932–) British

Eating People Is Wrong (Secker & Warburg, 1959). *Stepping Westward* (Secker & Warburg, 1965; Penguin, 1968). *The History Man* (Secker & Warburg, 1975).

BRAGG, Melvyn (1939–) British

For Want of a Nail (Secker & Warburg, 1965; Penguin, 1968). *The Second Inheritance* (Secker & Warburg, 1966; Penguin, 1968). *Without a City Wall* (Secker & Warburg, 1968; Penguin, 1970). *The Hired Man* (Secker & Warburg, 1969; Penguin, 1972). *A Place in England* (Secker & Warburg, 1970; Coronet, 1975). *The Nerve* (Secker & Warburg, 1971). *The Hunt* (Secker & Warburg, 1972). *Josh Lawton* (Secker & Warburg, 1972; Coronet, 1975). *The Silken Net* (Secker & Warburg, 1975).

BRAINE, John (1922–) British

Room at the Top (Eyre & Spottiswoode, 1957; Penguin, 1969). *The Vodi* (Eyre & Spottiswoode, 1959). *Life at the Top* (Eyre & Spottiswoode, 1962; Penguin, 1965). *The Jealous God* (Eyre & Spottiswoode, 1965; Pan, 1967). *The Crying Game* (Eyre & Spottiswoode, 1968; Pan, 1970). *Stay with Me Till Morning* (Eyre & Spottiswoode, 1970; Pan, 1972). *The Queen of a Distant Country* (Methuen, 1972; Pan, 1975). *The Pious Agent* (Eyre Methuen, 1975).

BROOKE-ROSE, Christine (1923–) British
The Languages of Love (Secker & Warburg, 1957). *The Sycamore Tree* (Secker & Warburg, 1958). *The Dear Deceit* (Secker & Warburg, 1960). *The Middlemen: A Satire* (Secker & Warburg, 1961). *Out* (Michael Joseph, 1964). *Such* (Michael Joseph, 1966). *Between* (Michael Joseph, 1968). *Go When You See the Green Man Walking* (Michael Joseph, 1970). *Thru* (Hamish Hamilton, 1975).

BROOKS, Jeremy (1926–) British
The Water Carnival (Eyre & Spottiswoode, 1957). *Jampot Smith* (Hutchinson, 1960). *Henry's War* (Macmillan, 1962).

BROPHY, Brigid (1929–) British
The Crown Princess, and Other Stories (Collins, 1953). *Hackenfeller's Ape* (Hart-Davis, 1953; Penguin, 1968). *The King of a Rainy Country* (Secker & Warburg, 1956). *Flesh* (Secker & Warburg, 1962). *The Finishing Touch* (Secker & Warburg, 1963). *The Snow Ball* (Secker & Warburg, 1964). *In Transit* (Macdonald, 1969).

BROWN, George Mackay (1921–) British
A Calendar of Love, and Other Stories (Hogarth Press, 1967). *A Time to Keep* (Hogarth Press, 1969), *Greenvoe* (Hogarth Press, 1972). *Magnus* (Hogarth Press, 1973).

BURGESS, Anthony (1917–) British
Time for a Tiger (Heinemann, 1956). *The Enemy in the Blanket* (Heinemann, 1958). *Beds in the East* (Heinemann, 1959). *The Right to an Answer* (Heinemann, 1960; New English Library, 1968). *The Doctor Is Sick* (Heinemann, 1960; Penguin, 1972). *The Worm and the Ring* (Heinemann, 1961). *Devil of a State* (Heinemann, 1961). *One Hand Clapping* [as Joseph Kell] (Davies, 1961). *A Clockwork Orange* (Heinemann, 1962; Penguin, 1972). *The Wanting Seed* (Heinemann, 1962; Penguin, 1973). *Honey for the Bears* (Heinemann, 1963; Penguin, 1973). *Inside Mr Enderby* [as Joseph Kell] (Heinemann, 1963; Penguin, 1966). *Nothing Like the Sun: A Story of Shakespeare's Love-Life* (Heinemann, 1964). *The Eve of Saint Venus* (Sidgwick & Jackson, 1964; New English Library, 1968). *The Long Day Wanes* (Norton, New York, 1966). *A Vision of Battlements* (Sidgwick & Jackson, 1965). *Tremor of Intent* (Heinemann, 1966; Penguin, 1969). *Enderby Outside* (Heinemann, 1968; Penguin, 1971). *Enderby* (Norton, New York, 1968). *Here comes everybody* (Faber, 1969). *MF* (Cape, 1971; Penguin, 1973). *The Clockwork Testament; or Enderby's End* (Hart-Davis, MacGibbon, 1974). *Napoleon Symphony* (Cape, 1974).

BURNS, Alan (1929–) British
Buster, in *New Writers One* (John Calder, 1961). *Europe after the Rain* (John Calder, 1965, pbk, 1967). *Celebrations* (Calder & Boyars, 1967; pbk, 1969). *Babel* (Calder & Boyars, 1969; pbk, 1972). *Dreamerika!* (Calder & Boyars, 1972). *The Angry Brigade* (Quartet Books, Allison & Busby, 1973).

BYATT, Antonia Susan (1936–) British
Shadow of a Sun (Chatto & Windus, 1964). *The Game* (Chatto & Windus, 1967; Panther, 1969).

CALLOW, Philip
A Pledge for the Earth (Heinemann, 1960). *Clipped Wings* (Gibbs & Phillips, 1964). *Flesh of Morning* (Bodley Head, 1971; Panther, 1973). *The Bliss Body* (MacGibbon & Kee, 1969). *Going to the Moon* (MacGibbon & Kee, 1968). *Yours* (Bodley Head, 1972; Quartet Books, 1974).

CARTER, Angela (1940–) British
Shadow Dance (Heinemann, 1966; as *Honeybuzzard*, Pan, 1968). *The Magic Toyshop* (Heinemann, 1967; Pan, 1969). *Several Perceptions* (Heinemann, 1968; Pan, 1970); *Heroes and Villains* (Heinemann, 1969; Pan, 1972). *Love* (Hart-Davis, 1971; Pan, 1972). *The Infernal Desire Machines of Doctor Hoffman* (Hart-Davis 1973; Panther, 1973).

CAUTE, David (1936–) British
At Fever Pitch (Deutsch, 1959; Quartet Books, 1973). *Comrade Jacob* (Deutsch, 1961; Quartet Books, 1973). *The Decline of the West* (Deutsch, 1966; Panther, 1968). *The Occupation* (Deutsch, 1971; Panther, 1972).

CLAYTON, Sylvia
Sabbatical (Faber, 1972). *Friends and Romans* (Faber, 1975).

COLE, Barry (1936–) British
A Run Across the Island (Methuen, 1968). *Joseph Winter's Patronage* (Methuen, 1969). *The Search for Rita* (Methuen, 1970). *The Giver* (Methuen, 1971). *Doctor Fielder's Common Sense* (Methuen, 1972).

COOPER, William (1910–) British
Trina [as H. S. Hoff] (Heinemann, 1934). *Rhea* [as H. S. Hoff] (Heinemann, 1937). *Lisa* [as H. S. Hoff] (Heinemann, 1937). *Three Marriages* [as H. S. Hoff] (Heinemann, 1946). *Scenes from Provincial Life* (Cape, 1950; Penguin, 1961). *The Struggles of Albert Woods* (Cape, 1952). *The Ever-Interesting Topic* (Cape, 1953). *Disquiet and Peace* (Macmillan, 1956). *Young People* (Macmillan, 1958). *Scenes from Married Life* (Macmillan, 1961). *Scenes from Life* (Scribner: New York, 1961). *Memoirs of a New Man* (Macmillan, 1966; Penguin, 1968). *You Want the Right Frame of Reference* (Macmillan, 1971). *Love on the Coast* (Macmillan, 1973).

DAVIE, Elspeth
Providings (Calder, 1965; pbk, 1969). *The Spark* (Calder & Boyars, 1969).

DAVIN, Dan (1913–) New Zealander/British
Cliffs of Fall (Nicholson & Watson, 1945). *For the Rest of Our Lives* (Nicholson & Watson, 1947). *The Gorse Blooms Pale* (Nicholson & Watson, 1947). *Roads from Home* (Michael Joseph, 1949). *The Sullen Bell* (Michael Joseph, 1956). *No*

Remittance (Michael Joseph, 1959). *Not Here, Not Now* (Hale, 1970). *Brides of Price* (Hale, 1972). *Breathing Spaces* [stories] (Hale, 1975).

DRABBLE, Margaret (1939–) British
A Summer Bird-Cage (Weidenfeld & Nicolson, 1963; Penguin, 1967). *The Garrick Year* (Weidenfeld & Nicolson, 1964; Penguin, 1971). *The Millstone* (Weidenfeld & Nicolson, 1965; Penguin, 1968). *Jerusalem the Golden* (Weidenfeld & Nicolson, 1967; Penguin, 1969). *The Waterfall* (Weidenfeld & Nicolson, 1969; Penguin, 1971). *The Needle's Eye* (Weidenfeld & Nicolson, 1972; Penguin, 1973). *London Consequences* [a group novel], ed. M. Drabble and B. S. Johnson; [the work also of Paul Ableman and others] (Greater London Arts Association, 1972). *The Realms of Gold* (Weidenfeld & Nicolson, 1975).

DRIVER, Charles Jonathan (1939–) South African/British
Elegy for a revolutionary (Faber, 1969; Penguin, 1971). *Send War in our Time, O Lord* (Faber, 1970). *Death of Fathers* (Faber, 1972). *A Messiah of the Last Days* (Faber, 1974).

DUFFY, Maureen (1933–) British
That's How It Was (Hutchinson, 1962). *The Single Eye* (Hutchinson, 1964). *The Microcosm* (Hutchinson, 1966). *The Paradox Players* (Hutchinson, 1967; Panther, 1969). *Wounds* (Hutchinson, 1969). *Love Child* (Weidenfeld & Nicolson, 1971; Panther, 1973). *I Want to go to Moscow: a lay* (Hodder & Stoughton, 1973). *Capital* (Cape, 1975).

DURRELL, Lawrence (1912–) British
Pied Piper of Lovers (Cassell, 1935). *Panic Spring* [as Charles Norden] (Faber, 1937). *The Black Book: An Agon* (Obelisk Press: Paris, 1938; Faber, 1973). *Cefalû* (Editions Poetry, 1947). *White Eagles over Serbia* (Faber, 1957). *Esprit de Corps; Sketches from Diplomatic Life* [stories] (Faber, 1957). *Stiff Upper Lip: Life Among the Diplomats* [stories] (Faber, 1958).
The Alexandria Quartet:
Justine (Faber, 1957; pbk, 1961). *Balthazar* (Faber, 1958; pbk, 1961). *Mountolive* (Faber, 1958; pbk, 1961). *Clea* (Faber, 1960; pbk, 1961).
The Dark Labyrinth (Faber, 1961). *Sauve Qui Peut* [stories] (Faber, 1966; pbk, 1969). *Aut Tunc Aut Nunquam: Tunc* (Faber, 1968). *Nunquam* (Faber, 1969; pbk, 1971). *Monsieur, or, The Prince of Darkness* (Faber, 1974). *The Revolt of Aphrodite* (Faber, 1974).

EDELMAN, Maurice (1911–75) British
A Trial of Love (Wingate, 1951). *Who Goes Home* (Wingate, 1953). *A Dream of Treason* (Wingate, 1954). *The Happy Ones* (Wingate, 1957). *A Call on Kuprin* (Longman, 1959). *The Minister* (Hamish Hamilton, 1961). *The Fratricides* (Hamish Hamilton, 1963). *The Prime Minister's Daughter* (Hamish Hamilton, 1964; Mayflower, 1974). *Shark Island* (Hamish Hamilton, 1967; Panther, 1969).

All on a Summer's Night (Hamish Hamilton, 1969). *Disraeli in Love* (Collins, 1972; Fontana, 1974). *Disraeli Rising* (Collins, 1975).

EKWENSI, Cyprian (1921–) Nigerian

People of the City (Dakers, 1954; Heinemann Educ., 1963). *Jagua Nana* (Hutchinson, 1961; Heinemann, 1975). *Burning Grass: A Story of the Fulani of Northern Nigeria* (Heinemann, 1962; Heinemann Educ., 1962). *Beautiful Feathers* (Hutchinson, 1963; Heinemann Educ., 1971). *The Rainmaker, and Other Stories* (African Universities Press, Lagos, 1965). *Iska* (Hutchinson, 1966; Panther, 1968). *Lokotown, and Other Stories* (Heinemann Educ., 1966). *Samankwe and the Highway Robbers* (Evan Bros., 1975).

ELLIOTT, Janice (1931–)

Cave with Echoes (Secker & Warburg, 1962). *The Somnambulists* (Secker & Warburg, 1964). *The Godmother* (Secker & Warburg, 1966). *The Buttercup Chain* (Secker & Warburg, 1967). *The Singing Head* (Secker & Warburg, 1968; Panther, 1971). *Angels Falling* (Secker & Warburg, 1969). *The Kindling* (Secker & Warburg, 1970). *A State of Peace* (Hodder & Stoughton, 1971; Coronet, 1973). *Private Life* (Hodder & Stoughton, 1972; Coronet, 1974). *Heaven on Earth* (Hodder & Stoughton, 1975).

FARRELL, James Gordon (1935–) British

A Man from Elsewhere (New Authors, 1963). *The Lung* (Hutchinson, 1965). *A Girl in the Head* (Cape, 1967; Pan, 1969). *Troubles* (Cape, 1970; Penguin, 1975). *The Siege of Krishnapur* (Weidenfeld & Nicolson, 1973; Penguin, 1975).

FEINSTEIN, Elaine

The Circle (New Authors, 1970; Penguin, 1973). *The Amberstone Exit* (Hutchinson, 1972; Penguin, 1974). *Children of the Rose* (Hutchinson, 1975).

FIELDING, Gabriel (1916–) British

Brotherly Love (Hutchinson, 1954). *In the Time of Greenbloom* (Hutchinson, 1956). *Eight Days* (Hutchinson, 1958). *Through Streets Broad and Narrow* (Hutchinson, 1960). *The Birthday King* (Hutchinson, 1962). *Gentlemen in Their Season* (Hutchinson, 1966). *Collected Short Stories* (Hutchinson, 1971).

FIGES, Eva (1932–) German/British

Equinox (Secker & Warburg, 1966; Pan, 1969). *Winter Journey* (Faber, 1967; Panther, 1969). *Konek Landing* (Faber, 1969; Panther, 1972). *B* (Faber, 1972). *Days* (Faber, 1974).

FITZGIBBON, Constantine (1919–)

The Arabian Bird (Cassell, 1949; Penguin, 1954). *The Iron Hoop* (Cassell, 1950). *Cousin Emily* (Cassell, 1952). *The Holiday* (Cassell, 1953). *When the Kissing had to Stop* (Cassell, 1960). *Going to the River* (Cassell, 1963). *High Heroic* (Dent, 1969). *In the Bunker* (Macmillan, 1973).

FORSTER, Edward Morgan (1879–1970) British

Where Angels Fear to Tread (Blackwood & Sons, Edinburgh, 1905; Penguin,

1969). *The Longest Journey* (Blackwood & Sons, Edinburgh, 1907; Penguin, 1971). *A Room with a View* (E. Arnold, 1908; Penguin, 1969). *Howards End* (E. Arnold, 1910; Penguin, 1969). *A Passage to India* (E. Arnold, 1924; Penguin, 1970). *Maurice* (E. Arnold, 1971; Penguin, 1975). *The Life to Come* [stories] (E. Arnold, 1972).

FORSTER, Margaret

Dame's Delight (Cape, 1964; World Distributors, 1966; Sphere, 1968). *The Bogeyman* (Secker & Warburg, 1965). *Georgy Girl* (Secker & Warburg, 1965). *The Travels of Maudie Tipstaff* (Secker & Warburg, 1967; Panther, 1970). *The Park* (Secker & Warburg, 1968; Panther, 1970). *Miss Owen—Owen is at home* (Secker & Warburg, 1969; Panther, 1970). *Fenella Phizackerley* (Secker & Warburg, 1969). *Mr. Bone's Retreat* (Secker & Warburg, 1971; Panther, 1974). *The Seduction of Mrs Pendlebury* (Secker & Warburg, 1974).

FOWLES, John (1926–) British

The Collector (Cape, 1958; Pan, 1965). *The Aristos* (Cape, 1965; Pan, 1968). *The Magnus* (Cape, 1966; Pan, 1968). *The French Lieutenant's Woman* (Cape, 1969; Panther, 1971).

FRAME, Janet (1924–) New Zealand

The Lagoon: Stories (Pegasus Press: Christchurch, N.Z., 1951). *Owls Do Cry* (W. H. Allen, 1961). *Faces in the Water* (W. H. Allen, 1962). *The Edge of the Alphabet* (W. H. Allen, 1962). *The Reservoir: Stories and Sketches, and, Snowman, Snowman: Fables and Fantasies* (Braziller: New York, 1963). *Scented Gardens for the Blind* (W. H. Allen, 1963). *The Adaptable Man*, (W. H Allen, 1965). *The Reservoir, and Other Stories* (W. H. Allen, 1966). *A State of Siege* (W. H. Allen, 1967). *The Rainbirds* (W. H. Allen, 1968). *Intensive Care* (W. H. Allen, 1971). *Daughter Buffalo* (W. H. Allen, 1973).

FRAYN, Michael (1933–) British

The Tin Men (Collins, 1965; Fontana, 1972). *The Russian Interpreter* (Collins, 1966). *Towards the End of the Morning* (Collins, 1967; Penguin, 1969). *A Very Private Life* (Collins, 1968; Penguin, 1971). *Sweet Dreams* (Collins, 1973).

FREEMAN, Gillian (1929–) British

The Liberty Man (Longman, 1955; Quartet Books, 1973). *Fall of Innocence* (Longman, 1956). *Jack Would Be a Gentleman* (Longman, 1959; Penguin, 1962). *The Leather Boys* [as Eliot George] (Blond, 1961; New English Library, 1967). *The Campaign* (Longman, 1963). *The Leader* (Blond, 1965). *The Alabaster Egg* (Blond, 1970). *The Marriage Machine* (Hamish Hamilton, 1975).

FULLER, Roy (1912–) British

The Second Curtain (Verschoyle, 1953). *Fantasy and Fugue* (Verschoyle, 1954; Penguin, 1970). *Image of a Society* (Deutsch, 1956). *The Ruined Boys* (Deutsch, 1959; Penguin, 1970). *Savage Gold* (Hutchinson, 1960). *The Father's Comedy* (Deutsch, 1961; Penguin, 1969). *The Perfect Fool* (Deutsch, 1963). *My Child, My Sister* (Deutsch, 1965). *The Carnal Island* (Deutsch, 1970).

GARNETT, David (1892–) British
Dope Darling [as Leda Burke] (Werner Laurie, 1919). *Lady into Fox* (Chatto & Windus, 1922). *A Man in the Zoo* (Chatto & Windus, 1924). *The Sailor's Return* (Chatto & Windus, 1925). *Go She Must!* (Chatto & Windus, 1927). *The Old Dovecote, and Other Stories* (Mathews & Marrot, 1928). *No Love* (Chatto & Windus, 1929). *The Grasshoppers Come* (Chatto & Windus, 1931). *A Terrible Day* (Joiner & Steele, 1932). *Pocahontas; or, the Nonpareil of Virginia* (Chatto & Windus, 1933). *Beany-Eye* (Chatto & Windus, 1935). *Aspects of Love* (Chatto & Windus, 1955; Penguin, 1959). *A Shot in the Dark* (Longman, 1958). *A Net for Venus* (Longman, 1959). *Two by Two: A Story of Survival* (Longman, 1963). *Ulterior Motives* (Longman, 1966). *An Old Master and Other Stories* (Yamaguchi Shoten, Tokyo, 1967). *A Clean Slate* (Hamish Hamilton, 1971). *The Starseekers* (Berkley, New York, 1971; Hale, 1975). *The Sons of the Falcon* (Macmillan, 1972; Quartet Books, 1973). *Plough Over the Bones* (Macmillan, 1973). *The Forgotten Dimension* (Hale, 1975). *The Master Cat: The True and Unexpurgated Story of Puss in Boots* (Macmillan, 1975). *Phantom Universe* (Hale, 1975).

GILLIATT, Penelope
One by One (Secker & Warburg, 1965). *A State of Change* (Secker & Warburg, 1967). *What's It Like Out?, and Other Stories* (Secker & Warburg, 1968). *Nobody's Business* (Secker & Warburg, 1972). *Sunday Bloody Sunday* (Secker & Warburg, 1972). *Unholy Fools* (Secker & Warburg, 1973).

GILLOTT, Jacky
Salvage (Gollancz, 1968; Penguin, 1971). *War Baby* (Gollancz, 1971; Penguin, 1974). *A True Romance* (Hodder & Stoughton, 1975).

GLANVILLE, Brian (1931–) British
The Reluctant Dictator (Werner Laurie, 1952). *Henry Sows the Wind* (Secker & Warburg, 1954). *Along the Arno* (Secker & Warburg, 1956), *The Bankrupts* (Secker & Warburg, 1958). *After Rome, Africa* (Secker & Warburg, 1959). *A Bad Streak, and Other Stories* (Secker & Warburg, 1961). *Diamond* (Secker & Warburg, 1962). *The Director's Wife, and Other Stories* (Secker & Warburg, 1963). *Goalkeepers Are Crazy: A Collection of Football Stories* (Secker & Warburg, 1964). *The Rise of Gerry Logan* (Secker & Warburg, 1963; Hodder pbks., 1970). *The King of Hackney Marshes, and Other Stories* (Secker & Warburg, 1965). *A Second Home* (Secker & Warburg, 1965; Pan, 1968) *A Roman Marriage* (Michael Joseph, 1966; Pan, 1969). *The Artist Type* (Cape, 1967; Pan, 1970). *The Olympian* (Secker & Warburg, 1969; Pan, 1972). *A Betting Man* (Coward McCann, New York, 1969). *A Cry of Crickets* (Secker & Warburg, 1970; Pan, 1972). *The Financiers* (Secker & Warburg, 1972). *The Comic* (Secker & Warburg, 1974).

GOLDING, William (1911–) British
Lord of the Flies (Faber, 1954; pbk, 1955; Penguin, 1960). *The Inheritors* (Faber, 1955; pbk, 1961). *Pincher Martin* (Faber, 1956; pbk, 1960). *Free Fall* (Faber,

1959; pbk, 1961). *The Spire* (Faber, 1964; pbk, 1965). *The Pyramid* (Faber, 1967; pbk. 1969). *The Scorpion God* (Faber, 1971; pbk, 1973).

GORDIMER, Nadine (1923–) South African

Face to Face: Short Stories (Silver Leaf Books, Johannesburg, 1949). *The Lying Days* (Gollancz, 1953). *The Soft Voice of the Serpent, and Other Stories* (Gollancz, 1953). *Six Feet of the Country* (Gollancz, 1956). *A World of Strangers* (Gollancz, 1958; Penguin, 1961). *Friday's Footprint, and Other Stories* (Gollancz, 1960). *Occasion for Loving* (Gollancz, 1963). *Not for Publication, and Other Stories* (Gollancz, 1965). *The Late Bourgeois World* (Gollancz, 1966). *A Guest of Honour* (Cape, 1971; Penguin, 1973). *Livingston's Companions* (Cape, 1972). *The Conservationist* (Cape, 1974).

GORDON, Giles (1940–)

Pictures from an Exhibition [short stories] (Allison & Busby, 1970). *The Umbrella Man* (Allison & Busby, 1971). *About a Marriage* (Allison & Busby, 1972; Penguin, 1974). *Girl with Red Hair* (Hutchinson, 1974; Wildwood House, 1974).

GREENE, Graham (1904–) British

The Man Within (Heinemann, 1929; uniform ed., 1952; Penguin, 1971). *The Name of Action* (Heinemann, 1930). *Rumour at Nightfall* (Heinemann, 1931). *Stamboul Train: An Entertainment* (Heinemann, 1932; Penguin, 1969). *It's a Battlefield* (Heinemann, 1934; Penguin, 1971). *England Made Me* (Heinemann, 1935; Penguin, 1970). *The Basement Room, and Other Stories* (Cresset Press, 1935). *The Bell Fell Free* (Grayson, 1935). *A Gun for Sale: An Entertainment* (Heinemann, 1936; Penguin, 1970). *Brighton Rock* (Heinemann, 1938; Penguin, 1970). *The Confidential Agent* (Heinemann, 1939; uniform ed., 1953; pbk, 1954; Penguin, 1969). *Twenty-four Stories*, [with James Laver and Sylvia Townsend Warner] (Cresset Press, 1939). *The Power and the Glory* (Heinemann, 1940; pbk, 1953; Penguin, 1969). *The Ministry of Fear: An Entertainment* (Heinemann, 1943; Penguin, 1970). *Nineteen Stories* (Heinemann, 1947). *The Heart of the Matter* (Heinemann, 1948; Penguin, 1969). *The End of the Affair* (Heinemann, 1951; Penguin, 1970). *The Third Man: An Entertainment* (Viking Press, New York, 1950). *The Third Man, and The Fallen Idol* (Heinemann, 1950; Heinemann Educ., 1972). *Loser Takes All: An Entertainment* (Heinemann, 1955; Penguin, 1971). *The Quiet American* (Heinemann, 1955; Penguin, 1969). *Our Man in Havana: An Entertainment* (Heinemann, 1958; Penguin, 1969). *A Visit to Morin* (privately printed, 1959). *A Burnt-out Case* (Heinemann, 1961; Penguin, 1970). *A Sense of Reality* (Bodley Head, 1963; Penguin, 1970). *The Comedians* (Bodley Head, 1966; Penguin, 1970). *May We Borrow Your Husband? and Other Comedies of the Sexual Life* (Bodley Head, 1967; Penguin, 1969). *Travels with My Aunt* (Bodley Head, 1969; Penguin, 1972). *The Honorary Consul* (Heinemann, Bodley Head, 1973; Penguin, 1975).

HANLEY, Gerald (1916–) British

Monsoon Victory (Collins, 1946). *The Consul at Sunset* (Collins, 1951; Mayflower, 1968). *The Year of the Lion* (Collins, 1953; Mayflower, 1969). *Drinkers of Darkness* (Collins, 1955; Penguin, 1958; Mayflower, 1968). *Without Love* (Collins, 1957). *The Journey Homeward* (Collins, 1961; Mayflower, 1969). *Gilligan's Last Elephant* (Collins, 1962; Mayflower, 1970). *See you in Yasukuni* (Collins, 1969).

HANLEY, James (1901–) British

The German Prisoner (privately printed, n.d.). *Drift* (Joiner and Steele, 1930). *A Passion Before Death* (privately printed, 1930). *The Last Voyage* (W. Jackson-Joiner & Steele, 1931). *Men in Darkness: Five Stories* (Lane, 1931). *Ebb and Flood* (Lane, 1932). *Stoker Haslett* (Joiner & Steele, 1932). *Aria and Finale* (Boriswood, 1932). *Captain Bottell* (Boriswood, 1933). *Resurrexit Dominus* (privately printed, 1934). *Quartermaster Clausen* (Arlan, 1934). *At Bay* (Grayson, 1935).

The Furys:

The Furys (Chatto & Windus, 1935). *The Secret Journey* (Chatto & Windus, 1936). *Our Time is Gone* (Lane, 1940). *Winter Song* (Phoenix House, 1950). *An End and a Beginning* (Macdonald, 1958).

Stoker Bush (Chatto & Windus, 1935). *Half an Eye: Sea Stories* (Lane, 1937). *Hollow Sea* (Lane, 1938). *People are Curious* (Lane, 1938). *The Ocean* (Faber, 1941; Macdonald, 1954). *No Directions* (Faber, 1941). *Sailor's Song* (Nicolson & Watson, 1943; Macdonald, 1953). *At Bay and Other Stories* (Faber, 1944). *Crilley and Other Stories* (Nicholson & Watson, 1945). *What Farrar Saw* (Nicholson & Watson, 1946). *Selected Stories* (Fridberg, Dublin, 1947). *Emily* (Nicholson & Watson, 1948). *A Walk in the Wilderness* (Phoenix House, 1950). *The House in the Valley* [as Patric Shone] (Cape, 1951). *The Closed Harbour* (Macdonald, 1952). *Collected Stories* (Macdonald, 1953). *Don Quixote Drowned* (Macdonald, 1953). *The Welsh Sonata: Variations on a Theme* (Verschoyle, 1954). *Levine* (Macdonald, 1956). *An End and a Beginning* (Macdonald, 1958). *Say Nothing* (Macdonald, 1962). *Another World* (Deutsch, 1972). *The Darkness* (Covent Garden Press, 1973). *A Woman in the Sky* (Deutsch, 1973).

HARRIS, Wilson (1921–) West Indian

The Guiana Quartet:

Palace of the Peacock (Faber, 1960; pbk, 1969). *The Far Journey of Oudin* (Faber, 1961). *The Whole Armour* (Faber, 1962). *The Secret Ladder* (Faber, 1963).

Heartland (Faber, 1964). *The Eye of the Scarecrow* (Faber, 1965; pbk, 1974). *The Waiting Room* (Faber, 1967). *Tumatumari* (Faber, 1968). *Ascent to Omai* (Faber, 1970). *The Sleepers of Roraima* (Faber, 1970). *The Age of the Rainmakers* (Faber, 1971). *Black Marsden* (Faber, 1972). *Companions of the Day and Night* (Faber, 1975).

HARTLEY, L. P. (1895–1972) British

Night Fears and Other Stories (Putnam, 1924). *Simonetta Perkins* (Putnam, 1925).

Killing Bottle [short stories] (Putnam, 1932). *The Shrimp and the Anemone* (Putnam, 1944). *The Sixth Heaven* (Putnam, 1946). *Eustace and Hilda* (Putnam, 1947; Faber, 1965). *The Boat* (Putnam, 1950). *The Travelling Grave, and Other Stories* (Barrie, 1951). *My Fellow Devils* (Barrie, 1951). *The Go-Between* (Hamilton, 1953; Penguin, 1958). *A White Wand, and Other Stories* (Hamish Hamilton, 1954). *A Perfect Woman* (Hamish Hamilton, 1955; Penguin, 1959). *The Hireling* (Hamish Hamilton, 1957; Penguin, 1973). *Facial Justice* (Hamish Hamilton, 1960). *Two for the River* [short stories] (Hamish Hamilton, 1961). *The Brickfield* (Hamish Hamilton, 1964; Sphere, 1969). *The Betrayal* (Hamish Hamilton, 1966; Sphere, 1969). *Poor Clare* (Hamish Hamilton, 1968). *The Collected Short Stories of L. P. Hartley* (Hamish Hamilton, 1968). *The Love-Adept : A Variation on a Theme* (Hamish Hamilton, 1969). *My Sister's Keeper* (Hamish Hamilton, 1970). *The Harness Room* (Hamish Hamilton, 1971). *Mrs Carteret Receives and Other Stories* (Hamish Hamilton, 1971). *The Collections* (Hamish Hamilton, 1972). *The Will and the Way* (Hamish Hamilton, 1973).

HEARNE, John (1926–) Jamaican
Voices under the Window (Faber, 1955, pbk, 1973). *Stranger at the Gate* (Faber, 1956). *The Faces of Love* (Faber, 1957; World Distributors, 1960). *The Autumn Equinox* (Faber, 1959). *Land of the Living* (Faber, 1961). *Fever Grass*, [with Morris Cargill (as John Morris)] (Collins, 1969). *The Candywine Development*, [with Morris Cargill (as John Morris)] (Collins, 1970).

HEPPENSTALL, Rayner (1911–) British
The Blaze of Noon (Secker & Warburg, 1939). *Saturnine* (Secker & Warburg, 1943; revised and extended version, as *The Greater Infortune* (Peter Owen, 1960; Sedgwick, 1964). *The Lesser Infortune* (Cape, 1953). *The Connecting Door* (Barrie and Rockliff, 1962). *The Woodshed* (Barrie and Rockliff, 1962; Calder & Boyars, 1968). *The Shearers* (Hamish Hamilton, 1969).

HIGGINS, Aidan (1927–) Irish
Felo de Se [stories] (John Calder, 1960). *Langrishe, Go Down* (Calder & Boyars, 1966). *Balcony of Europe* (Calder & Boyars, 1972).

HILL, Susan (1942–) British
The Enclosure (Hutchinson, 1961). *Do me a favour* (Hutchinson, 1961). *A Change for the Better* (Hamish Hamilton, 1969). *Gentlemen and Ladies* (Hamish Hamilton, 1969). *I'm the King of the Castle* (Hamish Hamilton, 1970; Penguin, 1974). *The Albatross, and Other Stories* (Hamish Hamilton, 1971). *Strange Meeting* (Hamish Hamilton, 1971; Penguin, 1974). *The Bird of Night* (Hamish Hamilton, 1972). *The Custodian* (Covent Garden Press, 1972; pbk, 1972). *In the Springtime of the Year* (Hamish Hamilton, 1974).

HINDE, Thomas (1926–) British
Mr Nicholas (MacGibbon & Kee, 1952; Penguin, 1962). *Happy as Larry* (MacGibbon & Kee, 1957). *For the Good of the Company* (Hutchinson, 1961). *A*

Place Like Home (Hodder & Stoughton, 1962). *The Cage* (Hodder & Stoughton, 1962). *Ninety Double Martinis* (Hodder & Stoughton, 1963). *The Day the Call Came* (Hodder & Stoughton, 1964; Coronet, 1974). *Games of Chance: The Interviewer and The Investigator* (Hodder & Stoughton, 1965). *The Village* (Hodder & Stoughton, 1966; Corgi, 1969). *High* (Hodder & Stoughton, 1968; Hodder pbks, 1970). *Bird* (Hodder & Stoughton, 1970; Coronet, 1972). *Generally a Virgin* (Hodder & Stoughton, 1972; Coronet, 1975). *Agent* (Hodder & Stoughton, 1974; Coronet, 1975). *Our Father* (Hodder & Stoughton, 1975).

HINES, Barry

The Blinder (Michael Joseph, 1966; Penguin, 1969). *A Kestrel for a Knave* (Michael Joseph, 1968; Penguin, 1969). *First Signs* (Michael Joseph, 1972). *Kes* (Michael Joseph, 1974).

HOWARD, Elizabeth Jane (1923–) British

The Beautiful Visit (Cape, 1950). *We are for the Dark: Six Ghost Stories* [with Robert Aickman] (Cape, 1951). *The Long View* (Cape, 1956). *The Sea Change* (Cape, 1959; Penguin, 1975). *After Julius* (Cape, 1965; Mayflower, 1968; Penguin, 1975). *Something in Disguise* (Cape, 1969). *Odd Girl Out* (Cape, 1972; Penguin, 1975). *Mr Wrong* [stories] (Cape, 1975).

HUGHES, Richard (1900–) British

A Moment of Time (Chatto & Windus, 1926). *A High Wind in Jamaica* (Chatto & Windus, 1929; Penguin, 1965). *In Hazard: A Sea Story* (Chatto & Windus, 1938; Penguin, 1950).

The Human Predicament:

I. *The Fox in the Attic* (Chatto & Windus, 1961). II. *The Wooden Shepherdess* (Chatto & Windus, 1972).

HUMPHREYS, Emyr (1919–) British

The Little Kingdom (Eyre & Spottiswoode, 1947). *The Voice of a Stranger* (Eyre & Spottiswoode, 1949). *A Change of Heart* (Eyre & Spottiswoode, 1951). *Hear and Forgive* (Gollancz, 1952; MacDonald, 1971). *A Man's Estate* (Eyre & Spottiswoode, 1955). *The Italian Wife* (Eyre & Spottiswoode, 1957). *Y Tri Llais* [in Welsh] (Llyrau'r Dryw, Llandybie, 1958). *A Toy Epic* (Eyre & Spottiswoode, 1958; Arrow Books, 1961). *The Gift* (Eyre & Spottiswoode, 1963). *Outside the House of Baal* (Eyre & Spottiswoode, 1965). *Natives* (Secker & Warburg, 1968). *National Winner* (Macdonald, 1971). *Flesh and Blood* (Hodder & Stoughton, 1974).

HYAMS, Edward (1910–)

The Wings of the Morning (Duckworth, 1939). *A Time to Cast Away* (Methuen, 1939). *To Sea in a Bowl* (Methuen, 1941). *William Medium* (Bodley Head, 1947). *Blood Money* (Bodley Head, 1948). *Not in our Stars* (Longmans Green, 1949). *The Astrologer* (Longmans Green, 1950). *Sylvester* (Longmans Green, 1951). *Gentian Violet: A Romance of Political Life* (Longmans Green, 1953). *Stories, and, Cream* (Longmans Green, 1954). *The Slaughterhouse Informer* (Longmans Green, 1955). *Into the Dream* (Longmans Green, 1957). *Taking it easy* (Longmans Green, 1958). *The Last Poor Man* (Longman, 1966). *A Perfect Stranger* (Longmans Green, 1964; Panther, 1968). *The Mischief-makers* (Longman, 1968). *The Final Agenda* (Allen Lane, 1973).

ISHERWOOD, Christopher (1904–) British/American
All the Conspirators (Cape, 1928). *The Memorial: Portrait of a Family* (Leonard & Virginia Woolf, 1932). *Mr Norris Changes Trains* (Hogarth Press, 1935; Penguin, 1969). *Sally Bowles* (Hogarth Press, 1937). *Goodbye to Berlin* (Hogarth Press, 1939; Penguin, 1969). *Prater Violet* (Methuen, 1946; Penguin, 1961). *The World in the Evening* (Methuen, 1954). *Down There on a Visit* (Methuen, 1962). *A Single Man* (Methuen, 1964; Penguin, 1969). *A Meeting by the River* (Methuen, 1967; Penguin, 1970).

JACOBSON, Dan (1929–) South African/British
The Trap (Weidenfeld & Nicolson, 1955; Penguin 1968 [with *A Dance in the Sun*]. *A Dance in the Sun* (Weidenfeld & Nicolson, 1956; see also *The Trap*). *The Price of Diamonds* (Weidenfeld & Nicolson, 1957; Penguin, 1968). *A Long Way from London* [stories] (Weidenfeld & Nicolson, 1958). *The Zulu and the Zeide* [stories] (Little Brown, Boston, 1959). *The Evidence of Love* (Weidenfeld & Nicolson, 1960). *Beggar My Neighbour* [stories] (Weidenfeld & Nicolson, 1964). *The Beginners* (Weidenfeld & Nicolson, 1966; Penguin, 1968). *Through the Wilderness* [stories] (Macmillan, New York, 1968). *The Rape of Tamar* (Weidenfeld & Nicolson, 1970; Penguin, 1973). *The Wonder-worker* (Weidenfeld & Nicolson, 1973).

JHABVALA, Ruth Prawer (1927–) British
To Whom She Will (Allen & Unwin, 1955). *The Nature of Passion* (Allen & Unwin, 1956). *Esmond in India* (Allen & Unwin, 1958). *The Householder* (Murray, 1960). *Get Ready for Battle* (Murray, 1962). *Like Birds, Like Fishes, and Other Stories* (Murray, 1963). *A Backward Place* (Murray, 1965). *A Stronger Climate: 9 Stories* (Murray, 1968). *An Experience of India* (Murray, 1971). *A New Dominion* (Murray, 1972). *Heat and Dust* (Murray, 1975).

JOHNSON, Bryan Stanley (1933–73) British
Travelling People (Constable, 1963). *Albert Angelo* (Constable, 1964). *Statement Against Corpses* [stories, with Zulfikar Ghose] (Constable, 1964). *Trawl* (Secker & Warburg, 1966; Panther, 1968). *The Unfortunates* (Secker & Warburg, 1969; Panther, 1969). *House Mother Normal* (Collins, 1971; Quartet Books, 1973), *Christie Malry's Own Double Entry* (Collins, 1972; Quartet Books, 1974). *Everybody knows Somebody Who's Dead* (Covent Garden Press, 1973). *See the Old Lady Decently* (Hutchinson, 1975).

JOHNSON, Pamela Hansford (1912–) British
This Bed Thy Centre (Chapman & Hall, 1935). *Blessed above Women* (Chapman & Hall, 1936). *Here Today* (Chapman & Hall, 1937). *World's End* (Chapman & Hall, 1937). *The Monument* (Chapman & Hall, 1938). *Girdle of Venus* (Chapman & Hall, 1939). *Too Dear for My Possessing* (Collins, 1940). *Tidy Death*, with Neil Stewart [as Nap Lombard] (Cassell, 1940). *The Family Pattern* (Collins, 1942). *Winter Quarters* (Collins, 1943). *Murder's a Swine*, with Neil Stewart [as Nap Lombard] (Hutchinson, 1943). *The Trojan Brothers* (Michael Joseph, 1944). *An Avenue of Stone* (Michael Joseph, 1947). *A Summer to Decide* (Michael Joseph, 1948; Penguin, 1954). *The Philistines* (Michael Joseph, 1949). *Catherine Carter* (Macmillan, 1952; Pan, 1957). *The Impossible Marriage* (Macmillan, 1954). *The Last Resort* (Macmillan, 1956). *The Humbler Creation* (Macmillan, 1959; Penguin, 1961). *The Unspeakable Skipton* (Macmillan, 1959; Penguin, 1961). *An Error of Judgement* (Macmillan, 1962). *Night and Silence! Who is there? An American Comedy* (Macmillan, 1963; Penguin, 1968). *Cork Street, Next to the Hatter's: A Novel in Bad Taste* (Macmillan, 1965; Penguin, 1968). *The Survival of the Fittest* (Macmillan, 1968; Penguin, 1970). *The Honours Board* (Macmillan, 1970). *The Holiday Friend* (Macmillan, 1972). *The Good Listener* (Macmillan, 1975).

JOHNSTON, Jennifer (1930–) Irish
The Captains and the Kings (Hamilton, 1972; Coronet, 1973). *The Gates* (Hamilton, 1973; Coronet, 1974). *How Many Miles to Babylon?* (Hamilton, 1974; Coronet, 1975).

JONES, Mervyn (1922–) British
No Time to Be Young (Cape, 1952). *The New Town* (Cape, 1953). *The Last Barricade* (Cape, 1953). *Helen Blake* (Cape, 1955). *On the Last Day* (Cape, 1958). *A Set of Wives* (Cape, 1965). *John and Mary* (Cape, 1966; Pan, 1969). *A Survivor* (Cape, 1968; Corgi, 1970). *Joseph* (Cape, 1970). *Mr Armitage Isn't Back Yet* (Cape, 1971; Quartet Books, 1973). *Holding On* (Quartet Books, 1973). *The Revolving Door* (Quartet Books, 1973). *Strangers* (Quartet Books, 1974). *Lord Richard's Passion* (Quartet Books, 1974).

JOSIPOVICI, Gabriel (1940–) British
The Inventory (Michael Joseph, 1968). *Words* (Gollancz, 1971). *Mobius the Stripper: Stories and Short Plays* (Gollancz, 1974). *The Present* (Gollancz, 1975).

KENEALLY, Thomas (1935–) Australian
The Place at Whitton (Cassell, 1964). *The Fear* (Cassell, 1965, Quartet Books, 1973). *Bring Larks and Heroes* (Cassell, 1967; Quartet Books, 1973). *Three Cheers for the Paraclete* (Angus & Robertson, Sydney, 1968; London, 1970; Penguin, 1969). *The Survivor* (Angus & Robertson, Sydney, 1969). *A Dutiful Daughter* (Angus & Robertson, 1971). *The Chant of Jimmie Blacksmith* (Angus & Robertson, 1972; Penguin, 1973). *Blood Red, Sister Rose* (Collins, 1974). *Gossip from the Forest* (Collins, 1975).

KING, Francis Henry (1923–) British

To the Dark Tower (Home & Van Thal, 1946; Arrow Books, 1975). *Never Again* (Home & Van Thal, 1948). *An Air That Kills* (Home & Van Thal, 1949). *The Dividing Stream* (Longmans Green, 1951). *The Dark Glasses* (Longmans Green, 1954). *The Firewalkers: A Memoir* (as Frank Cauldwell) (Murray, 1956). *The Widow* (Longmans Green, 1957; Penguin, 1961). *The Man on the Rock* (Longmans Green, 1958; Arrow Books, 1975). *So Hurt and Humiliated, and Other Stories* (Longmans Green, 1959). *The Custom House* (Longman, 1961). *The Japanese Umbrella, and Other Stories* (Longmans Green, 1964). *The Last of the Pleasure Gardens* (Longmans Green, 1965; Panther, 1968). *The Waves Behind the Boat* (Longmans Green, 1967; Arrow Books, 1975). *The Brighton Belle, and Other Stories* (Longmans Green, 1968). *A Domestic Animal* (Longman, 1970; Arrow Books, 1975). *Flights* (Hutchinson, 1973). *A Game of Patience* (Hutchinson, 1974). *The Needle* (Hutchinson, 1975).

KITCHEN, Paddy

Lying-in (Barker, 1965). *A Fleshly School* (Gollancz, 1970). *Paradise* (Gollancz, 1972).

LAMMING, George (1927–) Barbadian

In the Castle of My Skin (Michael Joseph, 1953; Longman, 1970). *The Emigrants* (Michael Joseph, 1954). *Of Age and Innocence* (Michael Joseph, 1958). *Season of Adventure* (Michael Joseph, 1960). *Water with Berries* (Longman, 1972). *Natives of My Person* (Longman, Caribbean: Port of Spain, 1972; Pan, 1974). *Cannon Shot and Glass Beads* (Pan, 1974).

LESSING, Doris (1919–) British

The Grass Is Singing (Michael Joseph, 1950; Penguin, 1961). *This Was the Old Chief's Country: Stories* (Michael Joseph, 1951).

Children of Violence:

Martha Quest (Michael Joseph, 1952; Panther, 1973). *A Proper Marriage* (Michael Joseph, 1954; Penguin, 1969). *A Ripple from the Storm* (Michael Joseph, 1958; Panther, 1969). *Landlocked* (MacGibbon & Kee, 1965; *The Four-Gated City* (MacGibbon & Kee, 1969; Panther, 1972).

Retreat to Innocence (Michael Joseph, 1956). *Five: Short Novels* (Michael Joseph, 1953; Penguin, 1960; Panther, 1974). *The Habit of Loving* (MacGibbon & Kee, 1957; Penguin, 1960). *The Golden Notebook* (Michael Joseph, 1962; Panther, 1973). *A Man and Two Women: Stories* (MacGibbon & Kee, 1963). *African Stories* (Michael Joseph, 1964; as *Winter in July*, Pan, 1966). *The Black Madonna* [stories] (Panther, 1974). *Briefing for a Descent into Hell* (Cape, 1971; Panther, 1972). *The Summer before the Dark* (Cape, 1973; Penguin, 1975). *The Memoirs of a Survivor* (Octagon, 1974).

LODGE, David (1935–) British

The Picturegoers (MacGibbon & Kee, 1960; Panther, 1970). *Ginger, You're Barmy* (MacGibbon & Kee, 1962; Panther, 1970). *The British Museum is Falling*

Down (MacGibbon & Kee, 1965). *Out of the Shelter* (Macmillan, 1970). *Changing Places: A Tale of Two Campuses* (Secker & Warburg, 1975).

LOWRY, Malcolm (1909–57) British
Hear us, O Lord, from Heaven Thy Dwelling Place (Cape, 1962; Penguin, 1969). *Ultramarine* (new ed. Cape, 1963; Penguin, 1974). *Under the Volcano* (Penguin, 1962; Cape, 1967). *Lunar Caustic*, ed. Earle Birnie and Margerie Lowry (Cape, 1968). *Dark as the Grave wherein my Friend is Laid*, ed. D. Day and Margerie Lowry (Cape, 1969; Penguin, 1972).

MACINNES, Colin (1914–) British
To the Victors the Spoils (MacGibbon & Kee, 1950; Panther, 1974). *June in Her Spring* (MacGibbon & Kee, 1952). *City of Spades* (MacGibbon & Kee, 1957; Panther, 1974). *Absolute Beginners* (MacGibbon & Kee, 1959; Panther, 1972). *Mr Love and Justice* (MacGibbon & Kee, 1960; Panther, 1974). *All Day Saturday* (MacGibbon & Kee, 1966; Panther, 1974). *Westward to Laughter* (MacGibbon & Kee, 1969). *Three Years to Play* (MacGibbon & Kee, 1970; Panther, 1971). *Out of the Garden* (Hart-Davis, MacGibbon, 1974).

MACKAY, Shena (1944–) British
Dust Falls on Eugene Schlumberger and *Toddler on the Run* (Deutsch, 1964). *Music Upstairs* (Deutsch, 1965; Panther, 1968). *Old Crow* (Cape, 1967; Panther, 1970). *An Advent Calendar* (Cape, 1971).

MANNING, Olivia
The Wind Changes (Cape, 1937). *Growing Up: A Collection of Short Stories* (Heinemann, 1948). *Artist among the Missing* (Heinemann, 1949). *School for Love* (Heinemann, 1951). *A Different Face* (Heinemann, 1953). *The Doves of Venus* (Heinemann, 1955). *My Husband Cartwright* (Heinemann, 1956).
The Balkan Trilogy:
The Great Fortune (Heinemann, 1960; Penguin, 1974). *The Spoilt City* (Heinemann, 1962; Penguin, 1974). *Friends and Heroes* (Heinemann, 1965; Panther, 1968; Penguin, 1974).
A Romantic Hero and Other Stories (Heinemann, 1967). *The Play Room* (Heinemann, 1969). *The Rain Forest* (Heinemann, 1974).

MARKANDAYA, Kamala (1924–) Indian
Nectar in a Sieve (Putnam, 1954). *Some Inner Fury* (Putnam, 1955; New American Library, 1970). *A Silence of Desire* (Putnam, 1960). *Possession* (Putnam, 1963). *A Handful of Rice* (Hamish Hamilton, 1966). *The Coffer Dams* (Hamish Hamilton, 1969). *The Nowhere Man* (Allen Lane, 1973). *Two Virgins* (Chatto & Windus, 1974).

MAUGHAM, Robin (1916–) British
The 1946 MS (War Facts Press, 1943). *The Servant* (Falcon Press, 1948). *A Line on Ginger* (Chapman & Hall, 1949). *The Rough and the Smooth* (Chapman & Hall, 1951). *Behind the Mirror* (Longmans Green, 1955). *The Man with Two Shadows*

(Longmans Green, 1958). *November Reef: A Novel of the South Seas* (Longmans Green, 1962). *The Green Shade* (Heinemann, 1966; New English Library, 1968). *The Second Window* (Heinemann, 1968; Pan, 1970). *The Link: A Victorian Mystery* (Heinemann, 1969). *The Wrong People* (Heinemann, 1970; Pan Books, 1973). *The Last Encounter* (W. H. Allen, 1972; Star Books, 1974). *The Black Tent and Other Stories* (W. H. Allen, 1972). *Testament—Cairo 1898* (*SS*) (Michael de Hartington, 1972). *The Barrier* (W. H. Allen, 1973). *Come to Dust* (W. H. Allen, 1973). *The Intruder* (W. H. Allen, 1974). *The Sign* (W. H. Allen, 1974).

McGAHERN, John (1934–) Irish
The Barracks (Faber, 1963). *The Dark* (Faber, 1965). *Nightlines* (Faber, 1970). *The Leavetaking* (Faber, 1974).

MIDDLETON, Stanley (1919–) British
A Short Answer (New Authors, 1958). *Harris's Requiem* (Hutchinson, 1960). *A Serious Woman* (Hutchinson, 1961). *The Just Exchange* (Hutchinson, 1962). *Two's Company* (Hutchinson, 1963). *Him They Compelled* (Hutchinson, 1964). *Terms of Reference* (Hutchinson, 1966). *The Golden Evening* (Hutchinson, 1968). *Wages of Virtue* (Hutchinson, 1969). *Apple of the Eye* (Hutchinson, 1970). *Brazen Prison* (Hutchinson, 1971). *Cold Graduations* (Hutchinson, 1972). *A Man Made of Smoke* (Hutchinson, 1973). *Holiday* (Hutchinson, 1974). *Distractions* (Hutchinson, 1975).

MITCHELL, Julian (1935–) British
Introduction, with others (Faber, 1960). *Imaginary Toys* (Hutchinson, 1961). *A Disturbing Influence* (Hutchinson, 1962). *As Far As You Can Go* (Constable, 1963). *The White Father* (Constable, 1964). *A Circle of Friends* (Constable, 1966; Panther, 1969). *The Undiscovered Country* (Constable, 1968; Panther, 1970).

MOORE, Brian (1921–) Canadian
Judith Hearne (Deutsch, 1955; Penguin, 1959). *The Feast of Lupercal* (Deutsch, 1958). *The Luck of Ginger Coffey* (Deutsch, 1960; Quartet Books, 1973). *An Answer from Limbo* (Deutsch, 1963; Quartet Books, 1973). *The Emperor of Ice-Cream* (Deutsch, 1966; Mayflower, 1967). *I Am Mary Dunne* (Cape, 1968; Penguin, 1973). *Fergus* (Cape, 1971). *Catholics* (Cape, 1972). *The Revolution Script* (Cape, 1972; Penguin, 1973). *The Great Victorian Collection* (Cape, 1975).

MORTIMER, Penelope (1918–) British
Johanna [as Penelope Dimont] (Secker & Warburg, 1947). *A Villa in Summer* (Michael Joseph, 1954). *The Bright Prison* (Michael Joseph, 1956). *Daddy's Gone A-Hunting* (Michael Joseph, 1958). *Saturday Lunch with the Brownings* (Hutchinson, 1960). *The Pumpkin Eater* (Hutchinson, 1962). *My Friend Says It's Bullet-Proof* (Hutchinson, 1967; Penguin, 1969). *The Home* (Hutchinson, 1971; Penguin, 1973). *Long Distance* (Allen Lane, 1974).

MOSLEY, Nicholas (1923–) British
Spaces of the Dark (Hart-Davis, 1951). *The Rainbearers* (Weidenfeld & Nicolson,

1955). *Corruption* (Weidenfeld & Nicolson, 1957). *Meeting Place* (Weidenfeld & Nicolson, 1962). *Accident* (Hodder & Stoughton, 1965). *Assassins* (Hodder & Stoughton, 1966; Penguin, 1969). *Impossible Object* (Hodder & Stoughton, 1968). *Natalie, Natalia* (Hodder & Stoughton, 1971; Penguin, 1975).

MURDOCH, Iris (1919–) British
Under the Net (Chatto & Windus, 1954; Penguin, 1960). *The Flight from the Enchanter* (Chatto & Windus, 1956). *The Sandcastle* (Chatto & Windus, 1957; Penguin, 1960). *The Bell* (Chatto & Windus, 1958). *A Severed Head* (Chatto & Windus, 1961). *An Unofficial Rose* (Chatto & Windus, 1962). *The Unicorn* (Chatto & Windus, 1963). *The Italian Girl* (Chatto & Windus, 1964). *The Red and the Green* (Chatto & Windus, 1965). *The Time of the Angels* (Chatto & Windus, 1966; Penguin, 1968). *The Nice and the Good* (Chatto & Windus, 1968; Penguin, 1969). *Bruno's Dream* (Chatto & Windus, 1969; Penguin, 1970). *A Fairly Honourable Defeat* (Chatto & Windus, 1970; Penguin, 1972). *An Accidental Man* (Chatto & Windus, 1971; Penguin, 1973). *The Black Prince* (Chatto & Windus, 1973; Penguin, 1975). *The Sacred and Profane Love Machine* (Chatto & Windus, 1974). *A Word Child* (Chatto & Windus, 1975).

NAIPAUL, V. S. (1932–) Trinidadian British
The Mystic Masseur (Deutsch, 1957). *The Suffrage of Elvira* (Deutsch, 1958; Penguin, 1969). *Miguel Street* (Deutsch, 1959; World Distributors, 1960). *A House for Mr Biswas* (Deutsch, 1961; Penguin, 1969). *Mr Stone and the Knights Companion* (Deutsch, 1963; Penguin, 1973). *The Mimic Men* (Deutsch, 1967; Penguin, 1969). *A Flag on the Island* [stories] (Deutsch, 1967; Penguin, 1975). *In a Free State* (Deutsch, 1971; Penguin, 1973). *Guerrillas* (Deutsch, 1975).

NAIPAUL, Shiva (1945–) Trinidadian
Fireflies (Deutsch, 1970). *The Chip-chip Gatherers* (Deutsch, 1973).

NARAYAN, R. K. (1907–) Indian
Cyclone, and Other Stories (Indian Thought Publications: Mysore, n.d.). *Swami and Friends: A Novel of Malgudi* (Hamish Hamilton, 1935). *The Bachelor of Arts* (Nelson, 1937). *The Dark Room* (Macmillan, 1938). *Malgudi Days* [stories] (Indian Thought Publications: Mysore, 1943). *The English Teacher* (Eyre & Spottiswoode, 1945). *An Astrologer's Day, and Other Stories* (Eyre & Spottiswoode, 1947). *Mr Sampath* (Eyre & Spottiswoode, 1949). *Dodu, and Other Stories* (Indian Thought Publications: Mysore, 1950?). *The Financial Expert* (Methuen, 1952). *Waiting for the Mahatma* (Methuen, 1955). *Lawley Road* [stories] (Indian Thought Publications, Mysore, 1956). *The Guide* (Methuen, 1958). *The Man-Eater of Malgudi* (Heinemann, 1962; New English Library, 1967). *Gods, Demons and Others* [stories] (Heinemann, 1965). *The Sweet-Vendor* (Bodley Head, 1967; Panther, 1970). *A Horse and Two Goats* [stories] (Bodley Head, 1970). *The Ramayana* (Chatto & Windus, 1973).

NEWBY, P. H. (1918–) British
A Journey to the Interior (Cape, 1945). *Agents and Witnesses* (Cape, 1947). *Mariner Dances* (Cape, 1948). *The Snow Pasture* (Cape, 1949). *The Young May Moon* (Cape, 1950). *A Season in England* (Cape, 1951). *A Step to Silence* (Cape, 1952). *The Retreat* (Cape, 1953). *The Picnic at Sakkara* (Cape, 1955). *Revolution and Roses* (Cape, 1957). *Ten Miles from Anywhere and Other Stories* (Cape, 1958). *A Guest and His Going* (Cape, 1959). *The Barbary Light* (Faber, 1962). *One of the Founders* (Faber, 1965). *Something to Answer For* (Faber, 1968). *A Lot to Ask For* (Faber, 1973).

NEWMAN, Andrea
Mirage (Bodley Head, 1965). *The Cage* (Blond, 1966; Panther, 1969). *Three Into Two won't go* (Macdonald, 1967; Pan, 1969). *Alexa* (Triton Books, 1969; Pan, 1970). *A Bouquet of Barbed Wire* (Triton Books, 1969).

NGUGI, J. (1938–) Kenyan
Weep Not, Child (Heinemann, 1964; pbk, 1965). *The River Between* (Heinemann, 1965). *A Grain of Wheat* (Heinemann, 1967).

NOONE, John (1936–) British
The Man with the Chocolate Egg (Hamish Hamilton, 1966; Penguin, 1972). *The Night of Accomplishment* (Hamish Hamilton, 1974).

NYE, Robert (1939–) British
Doubtfire (Calder & Boyars, 1967). *Tales I Told My Mother* (Calder & Boyars, 1969).

O'BRIEN, Edna (1932–) Irish
The Country Girls (Hutchinson, 1960; Penguin, 1963). *The Lonely Girl* (Cape, 1962; Penguin, 1964 [as *Girl with Green Eyes*]). *Girls in Their Married Bliss* (Cape, 1964). *August Is a Wicked Month* (Cape, 1965). *Casualties of Peace* (Cape, 1966; Penguin, 1968). *The Love Object* (Cape, 1968). *A Pagan Place* (Weidenfeld & Nicolson, 1970). *Night* (Weidenfeld & Nicolson, 1972).

O'FAOLAIN, Julia
We Might See Sights!, and Other Stories (Faber, 1968). *Godded and Codded* (Faber, 1970).

PLANTE, David (1940–) American/British
The Ghost of Henry James (Macdonald, 1970). *Slides* (Macdonald, 1971). *Relatives* (Cape, 1972). *The Darkness of the Body* (Cape, 1974).

POWELL, Anthony (1905–) British
Afternoon Men (Duckworth, 1931; Fontana, 1973). *Venusburg* (Duckworth, 1932; Penguin, 1961). *From a View to a Death* (Duckworth, 1933; Penguin, 1961; Fontana, 1968). *Agents and Patients* (Duckworth, 1936; Penguin, 1962). *What's Become of Waring* (Cassell, 1939; Penguin, 1962; Fontana, 1969).
A Dance to the Music of Time:

A Question of Upbringing (Heinemann, 1951). *A Buyer's Market* (Heinemann, 1952). *The Acceptance World* (Heinemann, 1955). *At Lady Molly's* (Heinemann, 1957; Fontana, 1969). *Casanova's Chinese Restaurant* (Heinemann, 1960; Fontana, 1970). *The Kindly Ones* (Heinemann, 1962). *The Valley of Bones* (Heinemann, 1964; Penguin, 1968; Fontana, 1973). *The Soldier's Art* (Heinemann, 1966; Fontana, 1968). *The Military Philosophers* (Heinemann, 1968). *Books Do Furnish a Room* (Heinemann, 1971; Fontana, 1972). *Temporary Kings* (Heinemann, 1973; Fontana, 1974). *Hearing Secret Harmonies* (Heinemann, 1975).

POWNALL, David

The Raining Tree War (Faber, 1974). *African Horse* (Faber, 1975).

PRIESTLEY, John Boynton (1894–) British

Adam in Moonshine (Heinemann, 1927). *Benighted* (Heinemann, 1927; Transworld, 1964). *Farthing Hall*, with Hugh Walpole (Macmillan, 1929). *The Good Companions* (Heinemann, 1929; Penguin, 1962). *Angel Pavement* (Heinemann, 1930; Penguin, 1964). *Faraway* (Heinemann, 1932). *I'll Tell You Everything*, [with Gerald Bullett] (Heinemann, 1933). *Wonder Hero* (Heinemann, 1933). *Four-in-Hand* [includes essays] (Heinemann, 1934). *They Walk in the City: The Lovers in the Stone Forest* (Heinemann, 1936; May Fair Books, 1961). *The Doomsday Men: An Adventure* (Heinemann, 1938; Transworld, 1963). *Let the People Sing* (Heinemann, 1939; Transworld, 1963). *Black-Out in Gretley: A Story of—and for—Wartime* (Heinemann, 1942). *Daylight on Saturday: A Novel about an Aircraft Factory* (Heinemann, 1943). *Three Men in New Suits* (Heinemann, 1945). *Bright Day* (Heinemann, 1946; Penguin, 1953). *Jenny Villiers: A Story of the Theatre* (Heinemann, 1947; Transworld, 1963). *Going Up: Stories and Sketches* (Pan, 1950). *Festival and Farbridge* (Heinemann, 1951). *The Other Place, and Other Stories of the Same Sort* (Heinemann, 1953). *The Magicians* (Heinemann, 1954). *Low Notes on a High Level: A Frolic* (Heinemann, 1954). *Saturn over the Water: An Account of His Adventures in London, South America and Australia by Tim Bedford, Painter* (Heinemann, 1961, pbk, 1963). *The Thirty-First of June: A Tale of True Love, Enterprise and Progress in the Arthurian and ad-Atomic Ages* (Heinemann, 1961). *The Shapes of Sleep: A Topical Tale* (Heinemann, 1962). *Sir Michael and Sir George: A Tale of COMSA and DISCUS and the New Elizabethans* (Heinemann, 1964). *Lost Empires: Being Richard Herncastle's Account of His Life on the Variety Stage from November 1913 to August 1914, Together with a Prologue and Epilogue* (Heinemann, 1965). *It's an Old Country* (Heinemann, 1967; Pan, 1970). *The Image Men: Out of Town and London End* (Heinemann, 1968; *Out of Town* and *London End*: Penguin, 1969). *The Carfitt Crisis, and two other stories* (Heinemann, 1975).

PRITCHETT, Victor Sawdon (1900–) British

Claire Drummer (Benn, 1929). *The Spanish Virgin, and Other Stories* (Benn, 1930). *Shirley Sanz* (Gollancz, 1932). *Nothing like Leather* (Chatto & Windus, 1935).

Dead Man Leading (Chatto & Windus, 1937). *You Make Your Own Life* (Chatto & Windus, 1938). *It May Never Happen, and Other Stories* (Chatto & Windus, 1945). *Mr Beluncle* (Chatto & Windus, 1951). *Collected Stories* (Chatto & Windus, 1956). *The Sailor, The Sense of Humor, and Other Stories* (Knopf: New York, 1956). *When My Girl Comes Home* (Chatto & Windus, 1961). *The Key to My Heart* (Chatto & Windus, 1963). *Blind Love, and Other Stories* (Chatto & Windus, 1969).

QUIN, Ann (1936–73) British

Berg (Calder & Boyars, 1964). *Three* (Calder & Boyars, 1966). *Passages* (Calder & Boyars, 1969). *Tripticks* (Calder & Boyars, 1972).

RAPHAEL, Frederic (1931–) American/British

Obbligato (Macmillan, 1956). *The Earlsdon Way* (Cassell, 1958; Penguin, 1961). *The Limits of Love* (Cassell, 1960). *A Wild Surmise* (Cassell, 1961). *The Graduate Wife* (Cassell, 1962). *The Trouble with England* (Cassell, 1962). *Lindmann* (Cassell, 1963). *Darling* (New American Library: New York, 1965). *Orchestra and Beginners* (Cape, 1967; Panther, 1970). *Like Men Betrayed* (Cape, 1970). *Who Were You with Last Night?* (Cape, 1971). *April, June and November* (Cape, 1972). *Richard's Things* (Cape, 1973). *California Time* (Cape, 1975).

RAVEN, Simon (1927–) British

The Feathers of Death (Blond, 1959; Panther, 1972). *Brother Cain* (Blond, 1959; Panther, 1974). *Doctors Wear Scarlet* (Blond, 1960; Panther, 1969). *Close of Play* (Blond, 1962; Panther, 1967).

Alms for Oblivion:

The Rich Pay Late (Blond, 1964; Panther, 1969). *Friends in Low Places* (Blond, 1965; Panther, 1969). *The Sabre Squadron* (Blond, 1966; Panther, 1972). *Fielding Gray* (Blond, 1967; Panther, 1969). *The Judas Boy* (Blond, 1968; Panther, 1969). *Places Where They Sing* (Blond, 1970; Panther, 1972). *Sound the Retreat* (Blond, 1971; Panther, 1974). *Come like Shadows* (Blond & Briggs, 1972; Panther, 1975).

Bring Forth the Body (Blond & Briggs, 1974).

READ, Piers Paul (1941–) British

Game in Heaven with Tussy Marx (Weidenfeld & Nicolson, 1966; Panther, 1968). *The Junkers* (Secker & Warburg, 1968; Panther, 1970). *Monk Dawson* (Secker & Warburg, 1969; Panther, 1971). *The Professor's Daughter* (Alison Press, 1971; Panther, 1973). *The Upstart* (Alison Press, 1973).

REDGROVE, Peter (1932–) British

In the Country of the Skin (Routledge, 1973). *The Terrors of Dr Treviles: A Romance* (Routledge, 1974).

REES, Barbara (1934–) British

Try another Country: Three novels (Secker & Warburg, 1969). *Diminishing Circles* (Secker & Warburg, 1970). *Prophet of the Wind* (Harcourt, 1973; New English Library, 1975).

RENAULT, Mary (1905–) British
Purposes of Love (Longmans Green, 1939). *Kind Are His Answers* (Longmans Green, 1940). *The Friendly Young Ladies* (Longmans Green, 1944). *Return to Night* (Longman, 1947). *North Face* (Longmans Green, 1948). *The Charioteer* (Longmans Green, 1953; New English Library, 1968). *The Last of the Wine* (Longmans Green, 1956). *The King Must Die* (Longmans Green, 1958; Four Square, 1961). *The Bull from the Sea* (Longmans Green, 1962; New English Library, 1968; Penguin, 1973). *The Mask of Apollo* (Longmans Green, 1966; New English Library, 1968). *Fire from Heaven* (Longman, 1970; Penguin, 1972). *The Persian Boy* (Longman, 1972; Penguin, 1974).

RICHLER, Mordecai (1931–) Canadian
The Acrobats (Deutsch, 1954; Sphere, 1970). *Son of a Smaller Hero* (Deutsch, 1955; Panther, 1972). *A Choice of Enemies* (Deutsch, 1957; Quartet Books, 1973). *The Apprenticeship of Daddy Kravitz* (Deutsch, 1959; Penguin, 1973). *The Incomparable Atuk* (Deutsch, 1963; Panther, 1972). *Cocksure* (Weidenfeld & Nicolson, 1968; Panther, 1969). *St Urbain's Horseman* (Weidenfeld & Nicolson, 1971; Panther, 1973). *The Street: Stories* (Weidenfeld & Nicolson, 1972).

ROOKE, Daphne (1914–) British/South African
A Grove of Fever Trees (Cape, 1951). *Mittee* (Gollancz, 1951). *Ratoons* (Gollancz, 1953). *Wizards' Country* (Gollancz, 1957). *Beti* (Gollancz, 1959). *A Lover for Estelle* (Gollancz, 1961). *The Greyling* (Gollancz, 1962). *Diamond Jo* (Gollancz, 1965). *Boy on the Mountain* (Gollancz, 1969). *Margaretha de la Porte* (Gollancz, 1974).

ROSS, Maggie
The Gasteropod (Barrie & Rockliff, 1968; Penguin, 1970). *Totem* (Covent Garden Press, 1973).

RUBENS, Bernice (1927–) British
Set on Edge (Eyre & Spottiswoode, 1960). *Madame Sousatzka* (Eyre & Spottiswoode, 1962). *Mate in Three* (Eyre & Spottiswoode, 1966). *The Elected Member* (Eyre & Spottiswoode, 1969; Penguin, 1971). *Sunday Best* (Eyre & Spottiswoode, 1971; Penguin, 1974). *Go Tell the Lemming* (Cape, 1973). *I Sent a Letter to My Love* (W. H. Allen, 1975).

ST OMER, Garth West Indian
A Room on the Hill (Faber, 1968). *Shades of Grey* (Faber, 1968). *Nor Any Country* (Faber, 1969). *J, Black Bam and the Masqueraders* (Faber, 1972).

SALKEY, Andrew (1928–) Jamaican
A Quality of Violence (New Authors, 1959). *Escape to an Autumn Pavement* (Hutchinson, 1960). *The Late Emancipation of Jerry Stover* (Hutchinson, 1968). *The Adventures of Catullus Kelly* (Hutchinson, 1969). *Come Home, Malcolm Heartland* (Hutchinson, 1972). *Anancy's Score* (Bogle-Louverture, 1973; pbk, 1973).

SANSOM, William (1912–) British

Fireman Flower (Hogarth Press, 1944). *Three* (Hogarth Press, 1946). *South: Aspects and Images from Corsica, Italy and Southern France* (Hodder & Stoughton, 1948; Penguin, 1952). *The Equilibriad* (Hogarth Press, 1948). *Something Terrible, Something Lovely* (Hogarth Press, 1948). *The Body* (Hogarth Press, 1949; Penguin, 1959; Sphere, 1968). *The Passionate North: Short Stories* (Hogarth Press, 1950). *The Face of Innocence* (Hogarth Press, 1951). *A Touch of the Sun* (Hogarth Press, 1952). *A Bed of Roses* (Hogarth Press, 1954). *Lord Love Us* (Hogarth Press, 1954). *A Contest of Ladies* (Hogarth Press:, 1956). *The Loving Eye* (Hogarth Press, 1956). *Among the Dahlias, and Other Stories* (Hogarth Press, 1957). *The Cautious Heart* (Hogarth Press, 1958). *The Last Hours of Sandra Lee* (Hogarth Press, 1961). *The Stories of William Sansom* (Hogarth Press, 1963). *Goodbye* (Hogarth Press, 1966). *The Ulcerated Milkman* [stories] (Hogarth Press, 1966). *The Vertical Ladder, and Other Stories* (Chatto & Windus, 1969). *Hans Feet in Love* (Hogarth Press, 1971). *A Young Wife's Tale* (Hogarth Press, 1974).

SARGESON, Frank (1903–) New Zealand

Conversations with My Uncle and Other Sketches (Unicorn Press: Auckland, 1936). *A Man and His Wife* (Caxton Press: Christchurch, 1940). *When the Wind Blows* (Caxton Press: Christchurch, 1945). *That Summer, and Other Stories* (Lehmann, 1946). *I Saw in My Dream* (Lehmann, 1949). *I for One* (Caxton Press: Christchurch, 1954). *Collected Stories, 1935–1963*, ed. Bill Pearson (MacGibbon and Kee, 1965). *Memoirs of a Peon* (MacGibbon and Kee, 1965). *The Hangover* (MacGibbon and Kee, 1967). *Joy of the Worm* (MacGibbon and Kee, 1969). *Man of England Now* [includes *A Game of Hide and Seek* and *I for One*] (Martin Brian and O'Keeffe, 1972).

SCOTT, Paul (1920–) British

Johnnie Sahib (Eyre & Spottiswoode, 1952; Mayflower, 1968). *The Alien Sky* (Eyre & Spottiswoode, 1953; Mayflower, 1968; Panther, 1974). *A Male Child* (Eyre & Spottiswoode, 1956; Mayflower, 1969; Panther, 1974). *The Mark of the Warrior* (Eyre & Spottiswoode, 1958; Pan, 1959; Mayflower, 1968). *The Chinese Love Pavilion* (Eyre & Spottiswoode, 1960; Panther, 1973). *The Birds of Paradise* (Eyre & Spottiswoode, 1962; Mayflower, 1969). *The Bender: Pictures from an Exhibition of Middle Class Portraits* (Secker & Warburg, 1963; Mayflower, 1969; Panther, 1975). *The Corrida at San Feliu* (Secker & Warburg, 1964). *The Jewel in the Crown* (Heinemann, 1966; Mayflower, 1968; Panther, 1973). *The Day of the Scorpion* (Heinemann, 1968; Mayflower, 1970; Panther, 1973). *The Towers of Silence* (Heinemann, 1971; Panther, 1973). *A Division of the Spoils* (Heinemann, 1975).

SELVON, Samuel (1923–) Trinidadian

A Brighter Sun (Wingate, 1952; Longman, 1972). *An Island is a World* (Wingate, 1955). *The Lonely Londoners* (Wingate, 1956; Brown, 1959 [as *The Lonely Ones*];

Longman, 1972). *Turn Again, Tiger* (MacGibbon & Kee, 1958). *Ways of Sunlight* (MacGibbon & Kee, 1958). *I Hear Thunder* (MacGibbon & Kee, 1963). *The Housing Lark* (MacGibbon & Kee, 1965). *The Plains of Caroni* (MacGibbon & Kee, 1970). *Those Who Eat the Cascadura* (Davis Poynter, 1972). *Moses Ascending* (Davis Poynter, 1975).

SHAW, Robert (1927–) British
The Hiding Place (Chatto & Windus, 1959; Penguin, 1962). *The Sun Doctor* (Chatto & Windus, 1961).
The Cure of Souls:
I. The Flag (Chatto & Windus, 1965; Penguin, 1968).
The Man in the Glass Booth (Chatto & Windus, 1967; Penguin, 1969). *A Card from Morocco* (Chatto & Windus, 1969).

SILLITOE, Alan (1928–) British
Saturday Night and Sunday Morning (W. H. Allen, 1958; Pan, 1960). *The Loneliness of the Long Distance Runner* (W. H. Allen, 1959; Pan, 1961). *The General* (W. H. Allen, 1960). *Key to the Door* (Macmillan, 1961). *The Ragman's Daughter* (W. H. Allen, 1963). *The Death of William Posters* (Macmillan, 1965). *A Tree on Fire* (Macmillan, 1967; Pan, 1969). *Guzman Go Home* (Macmillan, 1968). *A Start in Life* (W. H. Allen, 1970; Pan, 1972). *Travels in Nihilon* (W. H. Allen, 1971; Pan, 1973). *Raw Material* (W. H. Allen, 1972; Pan, 1974). *The Flame of Life* (W. H. Allen, 1974).

SINCLAIR, Andrew (1935–) British
The Breaking of Bumbo (Faber, 1959; Penguin, 1961). *My Friend Judas* (Faber, 1959). *The Project* (Faber, 1960). *The Hallelujah Bum* (Faber, 1963). *The Raker* (Cape, 1964). *Gog* (Weidenfeld & Nicolson, 1967; Penguin, 1970). *Magog* (Weidenfeld & Nicolson, 1972).

SNOW, C. P. (1905–) British
Death under Sail (Heinemann, 1932). *New Lives for Old* [published anonymously] (Gollancz, 1933). *The Search* (Gollancz, 1934).
Strangers and Brothers:
Strangers and Brothers (Faber, 1940; as *George Passant*, Penguin, 1973). *The Light and the Dark* (Faber, 1947; Penguin, 1962). *Time of Hope* (Faber, 1949; Penguin, 1970). *The Masters* (Macmillan, 1951; Penguin, 1956). *The New Men* (Macmillan, 1954; Penguin, 1970). *Homecomings* (Macmillan, 1956). *The Conscience of the Rich* (Macmillan, 1958; Penguin, 1961). *The Affair* (Macmillan, 1960; Penguin, 1970). *Corridors of Power* (Macmillan, 1964; Penguin, 1970). *The Sleep of Reason* (Macmillan, 1968; Penguin, 1970). *Last Things* (Macmillan, 1970; Penguin, 1972).
The Malcontents (Macmillan, 1972; Penguin, 1972). *In Their Wisdom* (Macmillan, 1974).

SOYINKA, W. (1934–) Nigerian
The Interpreters (Deutsch, 1965; Fontana, 1972). *Season of anomy* (Collings, 1973).

SPARK, Muriel (1918–) British
The Comforters (Macmillan, 1957). *Robinson* (Macmillan, 1958). *The Go-Away Bird, and Other Stories* (Macmillan, 1958). *Memento Mori* (Macmillan, 1959; Penguin, 1961). *The Ballad of Peckham Rye* (Macmillan, 1960; Penguin, 1970). *The Bachelors* (Macmillan, 1960). *The Prime of Miss Jean Brodie* (Macmillan, 1961; Penguin, 1969). *Voices at Play* [includes radio plays] (Macmillan, 1961). *The Girls of Slender Means* (Macmillan, 1963; Penguin, 1975). *The Mandelbaum Gate* (Macmillan, 1965; Penguin, 1970). *Collected Stories I* (Macmillan, 1967). *The Public Image* (Macmillan, 1968; Penguin, 1970). *The Driver's Seat* (Macmillan, 1970; Penguin, 1974). *Not to Disturb* (Macmillan, 1971; Penguin, 1974). *The Hothouse by the East River* (Macmillan, 1973; Penguin, 1975). *The Abbess of Crewe* (Macmillan, 1974; Penguin, 1975).

STOREY, David (1933–) British
This Sporting Life (Longmans Green, 1960; Penguin, 1962). *Flight into Camden* (Longmans Green, 1960). *Radcliffe* (Longmans Green, 1963). *Pasmore* (Longman, 1972). *A Temporary Life* (Longman, 1973).

TAYLOR, Elizabeth (1912–) British
At Mrs Lippincote's (Davies, 1945). *Palladian* (Davies, 1946). *A View of the Harbour* (Davies, 1947; Penguin, 1954). *A Wreath of Roses* (Davies, 1949; Penguin, 1967). *A Game of Hide-and-Seek* (Davies, 1951). *The Sleeping Beauty* (Davies, 1953). *Hester Lilly, and Other Stories* (Davies, 1954). *Angel* (Davies, 1957). *The Blush, and Other Stories* (Davies, 1958). *In a Summer Season* (Davies, 1961). *The Soul of Kindness* (Chatto & Windus, 1964). *A Dedicated Man, and Other Stories* (Chatto & Windus, 1965). *The Wedding Group* (Chatto & Windus, 1968; Penguin, 1970). *Mrs Palfrey at the Claremont* (Chatto & Windus, 1971). *The Devastating Boys* (Chatto & Windus, 1972).

TINDALL, Gillian (1938–) British
No Name in the Street (Cassell, 1959). *The Water and the Sound* (Cassell, 1961). *The Edge of the Paper* (Cassell, 1963). *The Youngest* (Secker & Warburg, 1967). *Someone Else* (Hodder & Stoughton, 1969). *Fly Away Home* (Hodder & Stoughton, 1971). *The Traveller and his Child* (Hodder & Stoughton, 1975).

TREVOR, William (1928–) Irish
A Standard of Behaviour (Hutchinson, 1958). *The Old Boys* (Bodley Head, 1964). *The Boarding House* (Bodley Head, 1965; Penguin, 1968). *The Love Department* (Bodley Head, 1966; Penguin, 1970). *The Day We Got Drunk on Cake, and Other Stories* (Bodley Head, 1967). *Mrs Eckdorf in O'Neill's Hotel* (Bodley Head, 1969; Penguin, 1973). *Miss Gomez and the Brethren* (Bodley Head, 1971). *The Ballroom*

of Romance (Bodley Head, 1972). *Elizabeth Alone* (Bodley Head, 1973). *The Last Lunch of the Season* (Covent Garden Press, 1973). *Angels at the Ritz, and Other Stories* (Bodley Head, 1975).

TUOHY, Frank (1925–) British
The Animal Game (Macmillan, 1957; Penguin, 1970). *The Warm Nights of January* (Macmillan, 1960). *The Admiral and the Nuns, and Other Stories* (Macmillan, 1962). *The Ice Saints* (Macmillan, 1964). *Fingers in the Door* (Macmillan, 1970).

TUTUOLA, Amos (1920–) Nigerian
The Palm-Wine Drinkard and His Dead Palm-Wine Tapster in the Dead's Town (Faber, 1952; pbk, 1962). *My Life in the Bush of Ghosts* (Faber, 1954; pbk, 1964). *Simbi and the Satyr of the Dark Jungle* (Faber, 1955). *The Brave African Huntress* (Faber, 1958). *Feather Woman of the Jungle* [stories] (Faber, 1962). *Abaiyi and His Inherited Poverty* (Faber, 1967).

VAN DER POST, Laurens (1906–) South African
In a Province (Hogarth Press, 1934). *The Face beside the Fire* (Hogarth Press, 1953). *A Bar of Shadow* (Hogarth Press, 1954). *Flamingo Feather* (Hogarth Press, 1955; Penguin, 1965). *The Seed and the Sower* [includes *A Bar of Shadow* and *The Sword and the Doll*] (Hogarth Press, 1963). *The Hunter and the Whale: A Tale of Africa* (Hogarth Press, 1967; Penguin, 1970). *A Story Like the Wind* (Hogarth Press, 1972). *A Far-off Place* (Hogarth Press, 1974). *A Mantis Carol* (Hogarth Press, 1975).

VANSITTART, Peter (1920–) British
I am the World: A Romance (Chatto, 1942). *Enemies* (Chapman & Hall, 1947). *The Overseer* (Chapman & Hall, 1949). *Broken Canes* (Bodley Head, 1950). *A Verdict of Treason* (Bodley Head, 1952). *A Little Madness: A London Story* (Bodley Head, 1953). *The Game and the Ground* (Reinhardt, 1956). *Orders of Chivalry* (Bodley Head, 1958). *The Tournament* (Bodley Head, 1959). *A Sort of Forgetting* (Bodley Head, 1960). *Sources of Unrest* (Bodley Head, 1962). *The Friends of God* (Macmillan, 1963). *The Lost Lands* (Macmillan, 1964). *The Dark Tower* (Macdonald, 1965). *The Shadow Land* (Macdonald, 1967). *The Story Teller* (Owen, 1968). *Pastimes of a Red Summer* (Owen, 1969).

WAIN, John (1925–) British
Hurry on Down (Secker & Warburg, 1953; Penguin, 1960). *Living in the Present* (Secker & Warburg, 1955). *The Contenders* (Macmillan, 1958; Penguin, 1969). *A Travelling Woman* (Macmillan, 1959). *Nuncle, and Other Stories* (Macmillan, 1960). *Strike the Father Dead* (Macmillan, 1962). *The Young Visitors* (Macmillan, 1965; Penguin, 1969). *Death of the Hind Legs, and Other Stories* (Macmillan, 1966). *The Smaller Sky* (Macmillan, 1967; Penguin, 1969). *A Winter in the Hills* (Macmillan, 1970; Penguin, 1974). *The Life Guard* (Macmillan, 1971).

WATERHOUSE, Keith (1929–) British
There is a Happy Land (Joseph, 1957; Longmans Green, 1968). *Billy Liar* (Joseph, 1959; Penguin, 1974). *Jubb* (Joseph, 1963). *The Bucket Shop* (Joseph, 1968).

WAUGH, Auberon (1939–) British
The Foxglove Saga (Chapman & Hall, 1960). *Path of Dalliance* (Chapman & Hall, 1963; Penguin, 1970). *Who Are the Violets Now?* (Chapman & Hall, 1965). *Consider the Lilies* (Michael Joseph, 1968). *A Bed of Flowers; or, As You Like it* (Michael Joseph, 1972).

WELDON, Fay (1933–) British
The Fat Woman's Joke (MacGibbon & Kee, 1967; Panther, 1969). *Down Among the Women* (Heinemann, 1971; Penguin, 1973). *Female friends* (Heinemann, 1975).

WHITE, Patrick (1912–) Australian
Happy Valley (Harrap, 1939). *The Living and the Dead* (Routledge, 1941; Penguin, 1967). *The Aunt's Story* (Routledge, 1948). *The Tree of Man* (Eyre & Spottiswoode, 1956; Penguin, 1970). *Voss* (Eyre & Spottiswoode, 1957). *Riders in the Chariot* (Eyre & Spottiswoode, 1961; Penguin, 1974). *The Burnt Ones* (Eyre & Spottiswoode, 1964; Penguin, 1968). *The Solid Mandala* (Eyre & Spottiswoode, 1966; Penguin, 1969). *The Vivisector* (Cape, 1970; Penguin, 1973). *The Eye of the Storm* (Cape, 1973).

WILSON, Angus (1913–) British
The Wrong Set, and Other Stories (Secker & Warburg, 1949; Penguin, 1961). *Such Darling Dodos, and Other Stories* (Secker & Warburg, 1950; Penguin, 1960). *Hemlock and After* (Secker & Warburg, 1952; Penguin, 1956). *Anglo-Saxon Attitudes* (Secker & Warburg, 1956; Penguin, 1958). *A Bit off the Map, and Other Stories* (Secker & Warburg, 1957). *The Middle Age of Mrs Eliot* (Secker & Warburg, 1958; Penguin, 1961). *The Old Men at the Zoo* (Secker & Warburg, 1961). *Late Call* (Secker & Warburg, 1964; Penguin, 1968). *No Laughing Matter* (Secker & Warburg, 1967; Penguin, 1969). *Death Dance: 25 Stories* (Viking Press, New York, 1969). *As If By Magic* (Secker & Warburg, 1973).

A select critical bibliography

Bernard Bergonzi *The Situation of the Novel*, Macmillan, 1970.

Malcolm Bradbury *Possibilities: Essays on the State of the Novel*, OUP, 1973.

Anthony Burgess *The Novel Now: A Student's Guide to Contemporary Fiction*, Faber, New ed., 1971.

Jonathan Culler *Structuralist Poetics: Structuralism, Linguistics and the Study of Literature*, Routledge & Kegan Paul, 1975.

Giles Gordon *Beyond the Words: Eleven Writers in Search of a New Fiction*, Hutchinson, 1975.

Gabriel Josipovici *The World and the Book: A Study of Modern Fiction*, Macmillan, 1971; pbk, Paladin, 1973.

Frank Kermode *Modern Essays*, Fontana, 1971. *The Sense of an Ending: Studies in the Theory of Fiction*, OUP, 1967.

David Lodge *Language of Fiction: Essays in Criticism and Verbal Analysis of the English Novel*, Routledge & Kegan Paul, 1966. *The Novelist at the Crossroads and other essays on fiction and criticism*, Routledge & Kegan Paul, 1971.

Robert Scholes *The Fabulators*, OUP, 1967.

Reference

James Vinson (ed.) *Contemporary Novelists*, St James Press: London, 1972; St Martins Press: New York, 1972.

Index